Workbook/Lab Manual to Accompany

Alles klar?

Second Edition

Karl F. Otto, Jr.
University of Pennsylvania

Wolff A. von Schmidt
University of Utah

Christine Goulding
California State University, Chico

Cindy Jorth
California State University, Chico

PEARSON
Prentice Hall

Upper Saddle River, NJ 07458

Publisher: Phil Miller
Acquisitions Editor: Rachel McCoy
Executive Marketing Manager: Eileen Moran
Asst. Director of Production: Mary Rottino
Assistant Editor: Meriel Martínez Moctezuma
Production Liaison: Claudia Dukeshire
Editorial and Production Supervision: Kathy Ewing
Prepress and Manufacturing Manager: Mary Ann Gloriande
Prepress and Manufacturing Buyer: Christina Helder
Line Art Manager: Guy Ruggiero

This book was set in TimesNewRomanPS 12/14 by Interactive Composition Corporation and was printed and bound by TCS. The cover was printed by TCS.

Some images © 2003 www.clipart.com.

© 2004, 1996 Pearson Education, Inc.
Upper Saddle River, NJ 07458

Printed in the United States of America
10 9 8 7 6 5 4 3 2 1

ISBN 0-13-182548-8

Pearson Education LTD., London
Pearson Education Australia PTY, Limited, Sydney
Pearson Education Singapore, Pte. Ltd.
Pearson Education North Asia Ltd., Hong Kong
Pearson Education Canada, Ltd., Toronto
Pearson Educación de México, S.A. de C.V.
Pearson Education – Japan, Tokyo
Pearson Education Malaysia, Pte. Ltd.
Pearson Education, Upper Saddle River, New Jersey

Table of Contents

Workbook

Table of Contents

Lab Manual

Preface

Because learning a language requires a great deal of practice, the *Workbook / Lab Manual to accompany Alles klar?* is an important tool for developing student proficiency. It provides students broad opportunities to reinforce what they are learning in class. Like the textbook, this supplement follows the premise that the most successful approach to language acquisition integrates structural and cultural learning with the development of learners' communicative skills. The *Workbook / Lab Manual*, therefore, provides additional practice in the four skills through both structured and open-ended activities. In addition, it includes activities that promote vocabulary acquisition and cultural understanding. It both is stimulating and informative, while also providing learners with the reinforcement of skills necessary to developing basic proficiency.

Because they use different media, the *Workbook* and *Lab Manual* appear as two separate entities within this volume. Each closely follows the sequencing of the main text, making it easy to assign activities related to class material.

The *Workbook* gives students ample practice in writing and reading, reinforces vocabulary from the chapter lists, and expands upon the language and cultural topics explored in the textbook. It allows students to practice in meaningful ways the themes, structures, and vocabulary they are learning in class. Specifically, each of the 12 *Workbook* chapters consists of five sections:

Themenwortschatz. Students use active vocabulary items from the *Themenwortschatz I* and *II* lists in context.

Schritte. Numerous activities in a wide range of formats, from structured to creative, offer contextualized practice of material learned in the textbook *Schritte.* Each task directs students to the appropriate section of the textbook chapter for reviewing pertinent material.

Alles klar? Like the *Alles klar?* section of each textbook chapter, this section of the *Workbook* contains activities that invite students to synthesize chapter themes and structures. Because the activities here are more open-ended, they encourage students to create their own meanings in German. The section also includes a reading selection or chart along with appropriate pre-reading or scanning activities. Beginning with *Kapitel 6,* these texts are drawn from authentic sources.

Kultur. Students explore aspects of German-speaking culture based on the chapter *Kulturnotiz* readings. Here they are often asked to analyze their own experiences as a basis for *understanding* rather than just *knowing about* the target culture. They compare and contrast what they learn about German culture with their own practices and cultures. In addition, the **Kultur** section contains activities that expand students' understanding of geography, idiomatic language use, and the German-speaking people and culture.

Erweiterung. This section helps further students' German skills by expanding on a theme or structure introduced in the text chapter or by offering students additional strategies for learning German.

The *Lab Manual* focuses on improving students' listening and speaking abilities. The *Lab Manual* is to be used in conjunction with the accompanying audio program which can be found on the Complete Audio on CD or online at the *Alles klar?* Companion Website (http://www.prenhall.com/allesklar/). In order to gain the most from the audio program, it is important that students respond *aloud* rather than silently when prompted to do so. Each of the 12 *Lab Manual* chapters includes four main sections:

Gespräche. Each of the dialogues that appear in the textbook is recorded by native speakers. In the *Hören Sie!* activities, students listen to the dialogues. In the *Wiederholen Sie!* section, students have the opportunity to repeat phrases during the pauses provided.

Aussprache. This section aids students with the pronunciation of the most difficult sounds in German for English-speakers. Chapters 1 through 9 address the sounds introduced in the *Versuch's mal!* section of the corresponding textbook chapter. Chapters 10 through 12 provide a review of all the sounds introduced in the first nine chapters. In addition to pronunciation activities, the poems and tongue twisters in the *Versuch's mal!* section of each textbook chapter are recorded here.

Strukturen. Students gain oral practice with the structures introduced in each chapter. Most activities provide immediate feedback or, where appropriate, correct answers are provided in the *Lab Manual Answer Key.*

Hörverständnis. Students listen to descriptions, narratives, or dialogues and complete activities that assess their comprehension. Correct answers are located in the *Lab Manual Answer Key.*

Level-appropriate practice and reinforcement are key to learning a language. When used as part of the *Alles klar?* program, the *Workbook / Lab Manual* can therefore contribute greatly to students' success in learning German.

Workbook

Kapitel 1

Grüß dich! Ich heiße . . .

Themenwortschatz

1-1 Assoziationen. What subjects of study do you associate with these things or people? Complete the crossword puzzle.

☞ REVIEW SCHRITT 2: Was studierst du? Ich studiere . . .

1. Kafka, Goethe, Novelle
2. *"Newsweek,"* "Der Spiegel," Artikel
3. Freud, Psychoanalyse, B. F. Skinner
4. Nietzsche, Kant, Existentialismus
5. Gesundheit, Medikamente, Doktor
6. Martin Luther, Katholizismus, Religion
7. Natur, Anatomie, Mikroskop
8. Demokratie, Präsident, Kommunismus
9. Nummer, Multiplikation, Algebra
10. Bach, Mozart, Orchester
11. Ozean, Kontinent, Land
12. Bauhaus, Hundertwasser, Rokoko

Schritte

1-2 Grüße. It's your first day as an exchange student at the Ludwig-Maximilians-Universität München. In your first course of the day, you meet some new people. Complete the exchanges.

☞ REVIEW SCHRITT 1: Wie heißt du? Ich heiße . . .

          SCHRITT 2: Was studierst du? Ich studiere . . .

          SCHRITT 3: Woher kommst du? Ich komme aus . . .

          SCHRITT 4: Wie geht's? Es geht mir . . .

INGE: Guten Morgen!

DU: (1) _____

INGE: Ich heiße Inge.

DU: (2) _____

ALBERT: Grüß dich! Wie heißt du?

DU: (3) _____

ALBERT: Was studierst du?

DU: (4) _____

DU: (5) _____

FLORIAN: Ich heiße Florian.

DU: (6) _____

FLORIAN: Mir geht's gut.

DU: (7) _____

FLORIAN: Ich komme aus Bonn.

DU: (8) _____

FLORIAN: Ich studiere Archäologie.

Erweiterung

Cognates

You have probably already noticed that German and English share many words that look or sound the same (cognates). Recognizing the patterns that exist between the two languages can often help you guess the meanings of many words in German that you have never seen before.

1-16 Urverwandte Wörter (*Cognates*). See if you can find the English cognates of the German words below. Use a German-English dictionary in your school library or use an online dictionary (links are located at the *Alles klar?* Companion Website). Begin by looking up the first three or four words in each set, then try to determine what letters you can substitute in the German words to arrive at the English cognates. You should recognize a pattern of letter correspondences in each set. Once you have found each correspondence, you should be able to guess most of the remaining words in each set. The first pattern is provided for you.

List the English cognate for each word. Remember that cognates are words that look and/or sound the same in both languages and have related meanings. When a word does not look familiar, saying it out loud may help.		The following German consonants often correspond to what consonant or consonant combination in their English cognates?
Pfeife: *pipe* Pfanne: *pan* helfen: Pfeffer:	reif: pflücken: Apfel: Bischof:	German **pf, f** often corresponds to English ___p___
Nacht: acht: hoch: recht:	Licht: lachen: Sicht: Fracht:	German **ch** often corresponds to English _____
Ding: Bruder: danken: dünn:	Feder: Bad: denken: dick:	German **d** often corresponds to English _____
Garten: trinken: Brot: Tropfen:	gut: selten: Bett: alt:	German **t** often corresponds to English _____
besser: Wasser: Fuß: sitzen:	Salz: Kessel: Katze: Zinn:	German **ss, ß, z, tz** often correspond to English _____
sieben: halb: Fieber: Weib:	lieben: Grab: Rabe: Kalb:	German **b** often corresponds to English _____

1-17 Analyse. Now speculate on the reasons for these lexical similarities between German and English. Can you think of any more German-English cognate pairs?

_____

_____

_____

_____

_____

_____

Recognizing these language similarities (and many others that will become apparent as you become more proficient), will not only make learning German easier but it can also give you new insights into the English language.

Kultur

2-14 Kulturnotizen. Briefly answer the following questions in English based on the **Kulturnotizen** sections of **Kapitel 2**.

1. What incentives does the German government provide for women to bear children? Why does the government offer such incentives? Does your own government provide similar incentives? Why or why not?

_____

_____

_____

_____

_____

_____

_____

2. Why do you think that Germany has one of the lowest birthrates in the world? What factors do you think contribute to this fact? How does the birthrate in your own country compare?

Single Children

The typical German family has only a single child. Recent studies have shown the number of children in German families to be approximately as shown below:

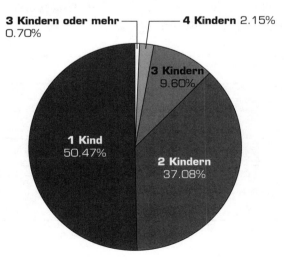

_____

_____

_____

_____

_____

_____

3. How does your own leisure time allotment compare to that of the Germans? Do you have more or less free time? Do you spend your free time doing similar or different things than the Germans?

_____

_____

_____

_____

_____

_____

_____

_____

4. German-Americans form the largest heritage group in the U.S; in fact, one-fourth of Americans have German ancestry. For what reasons have Germans immigrated to America over the centuries?

_____

_____

_____

_____

_____

_____

5. Where can you find traces of German immigration in your own town or state?

_____

_____

_____

_____

_____

_____

_____

2-15 Die Deutschen in Amerika. Immigrants from Central Europe have played an integral role in shaping America's past and present. Match the names of the following Americans of Swiss, Austrian, or German descent with the roles or products with which they are associated.

_____ 1. Albert Einstein   a. Autor

_____ 2. Dwight D. Eisenhower   b. Baseballspieler

_____ 3. Lou Gehrig   c. Industrielle und Philanthrop

_____ 4. Elvis Presley   d. Physiker

_____ 5. Grace Kelly   e. Präsident

_____ 6. Henry Kissinger   f. Sänger

_____ 7. John D. Rockefeller   g. Schauspielerin

_____ 8. John Steinbeck   h. Außenminister und Diplomat

_____ 9. John Jacob Bausch & Henry Lomb   i. Autos

_____ 10. Adolphus Busch   j. Bier

_____ 11. Walter Percy Chrysler   k. Brillen

_____ 12. Henry J. Heinz   l. Gold

_____ 13. Milton S. Hershey   m. Jeans

_____ 14. Heinrich Steinway   n. Ketchup

_____ 15. Levi Strauss   o. Klaviere

_____ 16. John Sutter   p. Schokolade

2-16 Ihre Deutschlandkenntnisse. On the following map of Germany, label the 16 German states (**Bundesländer**) and their capital cities (**Hauptstädte**). Use the map on the inside cover of *Alles klar?* to assist you.

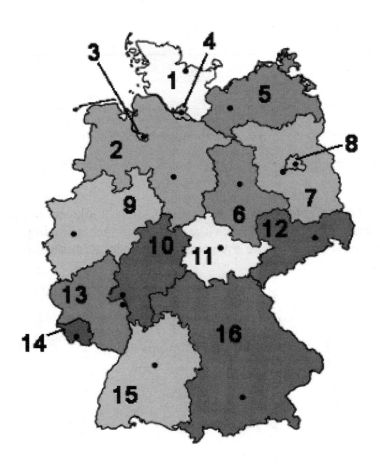

Bundesland – Hauptstadt

1. _____
2. _____
3. _____
4. _____
5. _____
6. _____
7. _____
8. _____

9. _____
10. _____
11. _____
12. _____
13. _____
14. _____
15. _____
16. _____

Erweiterung

Predicting noun genders and plurals

In **Schritt 6**, you learned that every noun in German has a gender and a specific plural form. While you must make memorizing these genders and plural forms part of learning your vocabulary, there are some patterns that allow you to predict the gender and/or plural form of a noun without having previously seen the word.

Here are some general observations about gender and plurals. Note that there are some exceptions to these generalizations.

	SUFFIXES	PLURAL FORMS
der	-ent, -ant, -ist **der Journalist, der Elefant, der Student**	-en **die Journalisten, die Elefanten, die Studenten**
	many with **-er** (especially ones that denote people) **der Kellner, der Mechaniker**	same as singular **die Kellner, die Mechaniker**
die	-schaft, -heit, -keit, -ung, -ei, -ion, -ik, -tät, -ur **die Grafik, die Verlobung, die Diskussion, die Landschaft, die Realität, dieTemperatur**	-en **die Graphiken, die Verlobungen, die Diskussionen, die Landschaften, die Realitäten, die Temperaturen**
	-ie **die Philosophie, die Garantie**	-n **die Philosophien, die Garantien**
	-in **die Kellnerin, die Amerikanerin**	-nen **die Kellnerinnen, die Amerikanerinnen**
	approximately 80% of nouns ending in **-e** are feminine (Remember: this means that 20% are not feminine!) **die Briefmarke, die Flöte, die Adresse** [But **der Junge, das Auge**]	-n **die Briefmarken, die Flöten, die Adressen** [**die Jungen, die Augen**]
das	-lein, -chen **das Fräulein, das Brötchen**	same as singular **die Fräulein, die Brötchen**
	-um, -ium **das Datum, das Gymnasium**	-(i)um changes to -(i)en **die Daten, die Gymnasien**
	-ment **das Instrument, das Element**	-e **die Instrumente, die Elemente**

2-17 Der, die, das, die. Predict the genders and plural forms of the following nouns, based on the tendencies described above. Do not look up the words until you have already guessed the genders. Some of these are cognates; others are formed from words that you have already learned and therefore have related meanings. What do you think they mean?

1. _____ Besucher, _____ _____

2. _____ Experiment, _____ _____

3. _____ Freundschaft, _____ _____

4. _____ Büchlein, _____ _____

5. _____ Studium, _____ _____

6. _____ Freiheit, _____ _____

7. _____ Mädchen, _____ _____

8. _____ Technologie, _____ _____

9. _____ Kommunist, _____ _____

10. _____ Kritik, _____ _____

11. _____ Musikerin, _____ _____

12. _____ Physiker, _____ _____

13. _____ Gesundheit (*no pl.*) _____ _____

14. _____ Dokument, _____ _____

15. _____ Tennisspieler, _____ _____

16. _____ Schönheit, _____ _____

17. _____ Information, _____ _____

18. _____ Museum, _____ _____

19. _____ Universität, _____ _____

20. _____ Sammler, _____ _____

What other words do you know that have the suffixes listed on the previous page?

_____

_____

_____

_____

_____

3-15 Kleinanzeigen (*Classifieds*). Read the following newspaper ads of furniture for sale. Don't be concerned if you don't understand every word. Find and list six items that you would like to buy.

Möbel

Zweisitzercouch, mod. Design, mint/schw., m. Chromfüssen, B. 1,75 m/H. 0,87 m/T. 0,86 m, €350,–; Tel. 040/45 81 76.

Guterh. Fernsehschrank, mass. Eiche, rustikal, dunkelbr., m. Videoteil ohne Rückwand, H 1,26 m/B 1 m/T 0,60 m; VB €500,–; Tel. 200 43 97.

Spiegelschrank, dunkelrot, 5 Türen, €250,–; franz. Bett m. Bettkasten, Matratze, €150,–; Tel. 544 067.

Tisch, 250x90, klassisch – High Tech, Platte: 30er Jahre. Beine: Stahl, roh ø 100 mm, VB 1.300,–. Tel. 220 45 85 abends.

Damen-Schreibtisch, Nussbaum, VB 500,–; Tel. 239 74 50.

Sofa-Klassiker, Eileen Gray, grau/schwarz, €1.250,–; Tel. 040/45 73 34, FAX: 040/45 76 78

Esstisch, rund, ø 90 cm., ausziehbar, m. 4 pass. Stühlen, Stck.–NP 1.200,–, zusammen m. Tisch €500,–; Tel. 86 23 50.

Kleiderschrank, weiß, mit 2 Spiegeltüren, B 1,00, H 2,00, T, 0,60 m, neu €300; 2 Bücherregale, weiß, B 0,70, H 1,75, T 0,25 m, je €55,–; 2 Tischlampen, Fuß goldenes Glas; günstig abzugeben; Tel. 040/81 76 34.

Seniorenbett, 2x1 m., Eiche hell, Taschenfederkern-Matratze, Nachttisch, pass. Stuhl, 10 Mon. alt, NP 2.200,–, jetzt 1300,–; Tel. 846 83 50.

1. _____   4. _____

2. _____   5. _____

3. _____   6. _____

Kultur

3-16 Kulturnotizen. Briefly answer the following questions in English based on the **Kulturnotizen** sections of **Kapitel 3**.

1. How does university student housing in Germany differ from that of the USA and Canada?

_____

_____

_____

_____

_____

_____

_____

2. What are the two most common housing options chosen by German students? Why?

_____

_____

_____

_____

_____

_____

_____

3. How are cars driven in Germany different than those in America? Why?

_____

_____

_____

_____

_____

_____

_____

_____

4. What are the various reasons that have prompted foreigners to relocate to Germany in the last fifty years? Name at least three. Do people immigrate to your country for similar reasons?

_____

_____

_____

_____

_____

_____

_____

3-17 Österreich: Geographie. How much do you know about the geography of Austria? On the map of Austria below, label each of the following places listed below. You may consult a map, if necessary.

Label the five largest cities: Wien, Graz, Linz, Salzburg, and Innsbruck
                three lakes: Neusiedler See, Wörther See, Bodensee
                three rivers: die Donau, der Inn, die Salzach

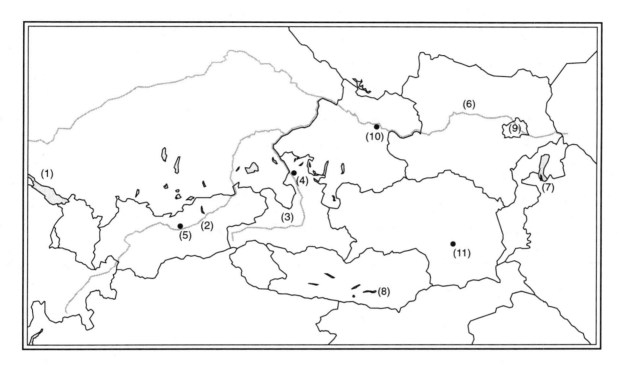

1. _____

2. _____

3. _____

4. _____

5. _____

6. _____

7. _____

8. _____

9. _____

10. _____

11. _____

3-18 Österreich: Assoziationen. Many people of Austrian origin, both past and present, have made an impact internationally. With what fields or items do you associate the following Austrian-born people?

_____	1. Sigmund Freud	a.	Autos
_____	2. Ferdinand Porsche	b.	Literatur
_____	3. Arnold Schwarzenegger	c.	Journalismus
_____	4. Christian Doppler	d.	Politik
_____	5. Wolfgang Amadeus Mozart	e.	Biologie
_____	6. Joseph Pulitzer	f.	Bankwesen
_____	7. Albert S. Rothschild	g.	Psychologie
_____	8. Gregor Mendel	h.	Filmkunst
_____	9. Kurt Waldheim	i.	Physik
_____	10. Ingeborg Bachmann	j.	Musik

What else do you associate with Austria, for example, foods, music, and so on?

_____

_____

_____

_____

_____

_____

Erweiterung

More on adjectives and adverbs

You have already seen the use of prefixes and suffixes in forming or modifying the meanings of adjectives.

zufrieden   *unzufrieden*
freund*lich*   *unfreundlich*

Being able to identify a root word—a verb, noun, or other adjective—can often help you guess the meaning of such an adjective. In the following list, you will see how three common suffixes, **-bar**, **-isch**, and **-lich**, are used to form adjectives. Note the type of words they can be combined with and the meanings that result from these combinations:

-bar
Combined with a verb, it is equivalent to the English *-able* or *-ible*:

essen   *to eat*   →   ess**bar**   *edible*
lesen   *to read*   →   les**bar**   *legible*

-isch
Combined with a noun, it indicates shared characteristics with the root person or thing:

Kind   *child*   →   kind**isch**   *childish*
Franzose   *Frenchman*   →   franzö**sisch**   *French*

-lich
Combined with a noun, it indicates similarity with the noun:

Freund   *friend*   →   freund**lich**   *friendly*
Bruder   *brother*   →   brüder**lich**   *brotherly*

combined with an adjective, it indicates a degree of the quality

grün   *green*   →   grün**lich**   *greenish*
froh   *happy*   →   fröh**lich**   *cheerful, merry*

combined with a verb, it indicates ability to do something

fragen   *to ask*   →   frag**lich**   *questionable, debatable*

Note that when forming adjectives from verbs, the suffixes are attached to the verb stem.

trinken   *to drink*   →   trink**bar**   *drinkable*

In addition, an umlaut is sometimes added to a word stem along with a suffix.

rot   *red*   →   röt**lich**   *reddish*

3-19 Endlich machbar! Find the English equivalent for each of the adjectives listed in the left-hand column.

_____ 1. ärztlich   a. audible

_____ 2. benutzbar   b. Austrian

_____ 3. beruflich   c. medical

_____ 4. bildlich   d. municipal, urban

_____ 5. essbar   e. professional

_____ 6. hörbar   f. visible

_____ 7. männlich   g. daily

_____ 8. österreichisch   h. paternal, fatherly

_____ 9. politisch   i. by phone

_____ 10. sachlich   j. usable

_____ 11. sehbar   k. objective, factual

_____ 12. spielerisch   l. edible

_____ 13. städtisch   m. pictorial, metaphorical, figurative

_____ 14. täglich   n. playful

_____ 15. telefonisch   o. political

_____ 16. väterlich   p. masculine

4-4 Um wie viel Uhr? Pick a day of the week and describe your normal routine for that day. Tell at what time you do each activity. Write out the times.

☞ REVIEW SCHRITT 3: Wie spät ist es?

BEISPIEL: Um halb zehn habe ich Biologie.

frühstücken	Abendessen kochen
Biologie / Deutsch / ? haben	arbeiten
schlafen gehen	von der Uni nach Hause gehen / fahren
zur Uni gehen / fahren	Kaffee trinken
essen	Hausaufgaben machen
?	

1. _____

2. _____

3. _____

4. _____

5. _____

6. _____

4-5 Geschenke. You've made New Year's resolutions for this year to do nice things for the people in your life. What will you do for whom? (Remember verb-second word order!)

☞ REVIEW SCHRITT 6:   The dative case / Indirect objects and Word order with two objects

WEM?		WAS?		AKTIVITÄT	
Mutter	Großeltern	Brief (*m.*)	CD (*f.*)	kaufen	geben
Vater	Schwester	Fahrrad (*n.*)	Buch (*n.*)	schenken	lesen
Freund	Professor	Zeitung (*f.*)	Schal (*m.*)	kochen	leihen
Partnerin	Mitbewohner	Abendessen (*n.*)	Blumen (*pl.*)	nähen	schicken
Arzt	Neffe	Gedicht (*n.*)	Schlittschuhe (*pl.*)	erzählen	schreiben
?		?		?	

BEISPIEL: Meinem Freund backe ich einen Schokoladenkuchen.
Ich erzähle meinen Nichten und Neffen viele Geschichten.

1. _____

2. _____

3. _____

4. _____

5. _____

6. _____

7. _____

8. _____

4-6 Wem? Fourteen-year-old Nicola is having a conversation with her mother. Complete the conversation with the correct dative personal pronouns.

☞ REVIEW SCHRITT 6: The dative case / Personal pronouns

NICOLA: Mutti, gibst du (1) _____ zwanzig Euro?

FRAU BEHRENS: Nein, so viel gebe ich (2) _____ nicht.

NICOLA: Warum denn nicht? Ankes Mutter gibt (3) _____ jede Woche zehn Euro.

FRAU BEHRENS: Ich bin nicht Ankes Mutter . . . . Warum willst du das Geld?

NICOLA: Anke und ich wollen ins Kino gehen.

FRAU BEHRENS: Das kostet ja keine zwanzig Euro!

NICOLA: Aber nach dem Film wollen wir essen gehen.

FRAU BEHRENS: Hör mal . . . Ich leihe (4) _____ zehn Euro für den Film, Nicola. Aber du musst (5) _____ nächste Woche das Geld wieder geben.

NICOLA: Aber wie kann ich mit zehn Euro beides (*both*) machen, den Film sehen und auch essen gehen?

FRAU BEHRENS: Ihr könnt nach dem Film nach Hause kommen und ich backe (6) _____ eine Pizza.

NICOLA: Na, gut. Machst du (7) _____ auch einen Salat? Nach dem Film haben wir bestimmt großen Hunger.

FRAU BEHRENS: Ja, aber kommt nicht zu spät nach Hause.

NICOLA: Danke, Mutti!

Alles klar?

4-15 Telefonat. Alexandra calls David to get some information about his brother Erwin. Read the telephone conversation and answer the following questions

ALEXANDRA: Tag, David. Wie geht's denn?

DAVID: Ach, ganz gut. Und dir?

ALEXANDRA: Auch gut. Sag mal, hat dein Bruder Erwin nicht im März Geburtstag?

DAVID: Nein, im Februar — das ist in zwei Wochen.

ALEXANDRA: Was macht ihr denn an seinem Geburtstag?

DAVID: Da kommen immer Freunde und Bekannte zu uns, und auch meine Familie.

ALEXANDRA: Und was schenkt ihm eure Familie zum Geburtstag?

DAVID: Das weiß ich nicht so genau. Aber ich weiß, er möchte eine Kamera.

ALEXANDRA: Na, schenkst du ihm die Kamera?

DAVID: Nein, das ist mir zu teuer. Vielleicht schenke ich ihm ein Buch.

ALEXANDRA: Moment mal! Ich habe eine Idee. Wollen wir ihm die Kamera zusammen kaufen?

DAVID: Nein, eine Kamera ist mir immer noch zu teuer. Außerdem liest er sehr gern. Ein Buch von Stephen King gefällt ihm bestimmt.

ALEXANDRA: Na, du hast Recht. Eine Kamera kostet zu viel. Vielleicht backe ich ihm einen Kuchen. Ich weiß, Schokoladenkuchen schmeckt ihm besonders gut.

DAVID: Ja, das kannst du machen. Dann kann ich auch ein Stück essen!

Fragen:

1. Wann hat Erwin Geburtstag?

   _____

2. Was möchte er zum Geburtstag?

   _____

3. Was will David seinem Bruder schenken?

   _____

4. Was will Alexandra für Erwin tun?

   _____

4-16 Abfahrt (*departure*) **und Ankunft** (*arrival*). Consult the following train schedule and write down at what time the trains depart from Karlsruhe and arrive in the various cities. Write out the times in words. The first one is done for you.

19.48 Karlsruhe Hbf

IC	19.56	"Mark Brandenburg"
		Offenburg 20.28 Freiburg (Brsg) Hbf 20.59 Basel Bad Bf 21.36 Basel SBB 21.43
	20.02	"Matterhorn"
		Mannheim Hbf 20.27 Mainz Hbf 21.16 Koblenz Hbf 22.05 Bonn Hbf 22.37 Köln Hbf 22.59 Düsseldorf Hbf
		23.31 Duisburg Hbf 23.44 Essen Hbf 23.57 Bochum Hbf 0.08 Dortmund Hbf 0.20
▲	20.03	✗ außer ⑥, nicht 10.VI., 1. XI., 24., 31. XII., 6. I.- Leopoldshafen 20.36 Hochstetten 20.47
	20.05	Graben-Neudorf 20.22 Hockenheim 20.39 Schwetzingen 20.47, weiter in Richtung Mannheim Hbf
E	20.08	Rastatt 20.20 Baden-Baden 20.26 Bühl (Baden) 20.35 Achern 20.42 Appenweier 20.53
D	20.09	Bruchsal 20.22 Heidelberg Hbf 20.42 Darmstadt Hbf 21.24 Frankfurt (Main) Hbf 21.54 Offenbach(Main)
		Hbf 22.24 Hanau Hbf 22.34 Fulda 23.28 Bad Hersfeld 23.57 Bebra 0.08 Eisenach 1.04 Gotha 1.30 Erfurt
		Hbf 1.55 Weimar 2.24 Naumburg (Salle) Hbf 2.53 Leipzig Hbf 3.33 Riesa 4.25 Dresden-Neustadt 5.03
		Dresden Hbf 5.11
	20.14	✗ außer ⑥, nicht 10. VI., 1. XI., 24., 31. XII., 6. I. in Richtung Rastatt über Muggensturm
E	20.18	-täglich außer ⑥, nicht 24., 31. XII., auch 25. XII., 1, 1.- Bretten Bf 20.39
▲	20.19	Ettlingen Stadt 20.34 Bad Herrenalb 20.56
▲	20.23	Leopoldshafen 20.56
RSB	20.26	-täglich außer ⑥, nicht 24., 31. XII., auch 25. XII., 1. I.- Karlsruhe-Mühlburg 20-31 Würth (Rhein) 20.37
		Kandel 20.44 Winden (Pfalz) 20.50 Landau (Pfalz) Hbf 20.59, weiter in Richtung Neustadt (Weinstr) Hbf
	20.26	✗ außer ⑥, nicht 10. VI., 1. XI., 24., 31. XII., 6. I. - Bruchsal 20.46

▲ = ab Bahnhofsvorplatz

VON KARLSRUHE	ABFAHRT	ANKUNFT
nach Mannheim	um zwanzig Uhr zwei	um zwanzig Uhr siebenundzwanzig
nach Basel SBB		
nach Leipzig		
nach Koblenz		
nach Weimar		

4-17 Hedwigs Woche. Hedwig has a busy schedule. Examine the page from her calendar, then write a paragraph about her activities for the week. Include phrases like **jeden Tag**, **am Wochenende**, and so on. Write at least eight sentences.

Mo	Di	Mi	Do	Fr	Sa	So
7.00 zu Hause frühstücken					länger schlafen!	
8.30 zur Arbeit fahren					9.00 frühstücken, Zeitung lesen	
9.00–12.00 Arbeit					9.45 nach Biel fahren	10.00 mit Petra Tennis spielen
	13.00 mit Karin essen		14.30 zum Arzt gehen	15.30 das Auto waschen	16.00 nach Hause kommen	14.30 Mutti besuchen, ihr mit der Gartenarbeit helfen
joggen						
18.30 Abendessen zu Hause					19.00 Abendessen bei Gustav	
20.00 E-mails schreiben			20.00 E-mails schreiben			
23.00 ins Bett gehen						

_____

_____

_____

_____

_____

_____

_____

_____

4-18 Meine Woche. Now write a paragraph about your own activities during a typical week in your life. Include phrases like **jeden Tag**, **am Wochenende**, and so on. Use coordinating conjunctions to vary your sentence lengths and make your writing more interesting. Write at least eight sentences.

_____

_____

_____

_____

_____

_____

_____

_____

_____

Kultur

4-19 Kulturnotizen. Briefly answer the following questions in English based on the **Kulturnotizen** sections of **Kapitel 4**.

1. What are the similarities and differences between birthday customs in your country and those of the Germans?

   _____

   _____

   _____

   _____

   _____

   _____

   _____

2. Explain why the performing arts are a local enterprise in the German-speaking countries. What are the advantages and disadvantages of such a system? How are the arts supported and what role do they play in your country?

   _____

   _____

   _____

   _____

   _____

   _____

   _____

   _____

3. What is the average annual temperature in the German-speaking regions of Europe? How does the climate of Central Europe compare with the climate of your own region?

   _____

   _____

   _____

   _____

   _____

_____

_____

_____

4. Describe the geopolitical position of Switzerland in Europe. What features and policies set it apart from most other European nations?

_____

_____

_____

_____

_____

_____

_____

_____

4-20 Die Schweiz: Geographie. How much do you know about the geography of Switzerland? On the map of Switzerland below, label each of the following places listed below. You may consult a map, if necessary.

Label: the 5 largest cities: Zürich, Genf, Basel, Bern, and Lausanne.
       4 lakes: Genfer See, Bodensee, Zürichsee, Vierwaldstättersee
       3 rivers: der Rhein, die Rhône, der Inn
       4 mountain peaks: Dom, Dufourspitze (Monte Rosa), Jungfrau, Matterhorn

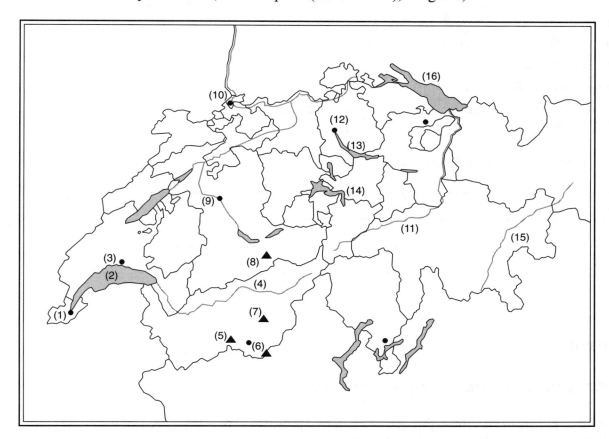

1. _____   9. _____

2. _____   10. _____

3. _____   11. _____

4. _____   12. _____

5. _____   13. _____

6. _____   14. _____

7. _____   15. _____

8. _____   16. _____

4-21 Die Schweiz: Assoziationen. Many people of Swiss origin, both past and present, have made an impact internationally. With what fields or items do you associate the following Swiss-born people?

_____	1. Louis Chevrolet	a.	Autos
_____	2. Martina Hingis	b.	Kunst
_____	3. Carl Gustav Jung	c.	Linguistik
_____	4. Paul Klee	d.	Medizin
_____	5. Paracelsus	e.	Philosophie
_____	6. Johann Heinrich Pestalozzi	f.	Protestantismus
_____	7. Hermann Rorschach	g.	Psychiatrie
_____	8. Jean-Jacques Rousseau	h.	Psychologie
_____	9. Ferdinand de Saussure	i.	Schulreform
_____	10. Ulrich Zwingli	j.	Tennis

What else do you associate with Switzerland?

_____

_____

_____

_____

Erweiterung

Idiomatic expressions using the dative

There are several phrases in German that require a dative personal pronoun where English uses a subject pronoun. You learned a few of these in Kapitel 1:

Wie geht es **dir (Ihnen, ihm)**?	How are you [*sing. fam.*] (you [*form.*], is he) doing?
Es geht **mir (dir, ihm)** gut / schlecht.	I am (You are, He is) well / not well.
Es tut **mir (dir, ihm)** Leid.	I am (You are, He is) sorry.

Here are some other expressions that require a dative personal pronoun:

Es ist **mir (dir, ihm)** kalt / heiß.	I am (You are, He is) cold / hot.
Es ist **mir (dir, ihm)** egal.	I don't (You don't, He doesn't) care.
Das ist **mir (dir, ihm)** zu teuer / groß.	That's too expensive / large for my (your, his) taste.
Das ist **mir (dir, ihm)** wichtig / peinlich / fremd / nützlich.	That's important / embarrassing / foreign / useful to me (you, him).
Das bedeutet **mir (dir, ihm)** nichts.	That means nothing to me (you, him).

4-22 Wie, bitte? What might you say in the following situations?

1. Sie campen in den Alpen. Es schneit und Sie frieren.

   _____

2. Sie möchten Ihren Professor für Deutsch nach seiner Gesundheit fragen.

   _____

3. Ihr Professor sagt Ihnen, er ist krank.

   _____

4. Sie möchten ein neues Handy, aber es kostet jeden Monat €99 und so viel haben Sie nicht.

   _____

5. Sie kommen gerade aus der Toilette und Sie haben Toilettenpapier unter Ihrem Schuh.

   _____

4-23 Wie sagt man das auf Deutsch? Translate the following sentences into idiomatic German.

1. The car is too expensive for him.

   _____

2. We're very sorry!

   _____

3. Her family is important to her.

   _____

4. You (*fam., pl.*) don't care.

   _____

5. They are too hot.

   _____

> **Wie du mir, so ich dir.**
> *Tit for tat.*

Kapitel 5

Wie und wo wohnen wir?

Themenwortschatz

5-1 Zu Hause. What furniture or other items is one likely to find in each of the following rooms? List at least three different items per room. Be sure to include the correct article with each item.

BEISPIEL: im Esszimmer: der Esstisch, die Stühle, der Teppich

in der Küche: _____

im Schlafzimmer: _____

im Wohnzimmer: _____

im Arbeitszimmer: _____

im Bad: _____

in der Garage: _____

5-2 Wo macht man das? Now list at least two activities that one typically does in each of the following rooms. List the verbs in their infinitive forms.

BEISPIEL: im Bad: die Toilette sauber machen, duschen

in der Küche: _____

im Schlafzimmer: _____

im Wohnzimmer: _____

im Arbeitszimmer: _____

im Esszimmer: _____

in der Garage: _____

Schritte

5-3 Wo ich wohne. Jot down some notes about your current living situation, using the cues provided.

☞ REVIEW SCHRITT 1: Ich wohne . . .
        SCHRITT 2: Meine Wohnung hat . . .
        SCHRITT 3: Meine Wohnung ist . . .

Wie viele Stockwerke? _____

Welche Zimmer? _____

Welche Möbel? _____

Mitbewohner(innen)? _____

Wie ist die Wohnung? (Adjektive) _____

Now describe your living situation: where and with whom you live, what the house / apartment / room is like, what you have in it, and so on. Write at least eight sentences.

_____

_____

_____

_____

_____

_____

_____

_____

_____

5-7 Mein Auto. Complete Niels and Barbara's conversation with the correct forms of the verbs **wissen**, **kennen**, or **können**.

☞ REVIEW SCHRITT 6: **wissen / kennen / können**

NIELS: Mein Auto ist kaputt, und ich (1) _____ nicht, was los ist.

(2) _____ du, was ich machen soll?

BARBARA: Ich (3) _____ nicht so viel über Autos, aber vielleicht

(4) _____ ich dir helfen. Ich (5) _____ einen guten Mechaniker.

NIELS: Tatsächlich! Woher (6) _____ du ihn?

BARBARA: Ich (7) _____ ihn schon seit Jahren — er ist mein Vetter! Er repariert

immer das Auto von meinen Eltern. Ich (8) _____ ihn sehr

empfehlen, denn er (9) _____ sehr viel über Autos.

NIELS: Wo (10) _____ ich ihn finden?

BARBARA: Hier ist seine Telefonnummer. Er (11) _____ dir sicher helfen.

NIELS: Danke!

5-8 Saras neue Wohnung. Niels is telling Sonja about Sara's recent move. Underline the auxiliary verbs and past participles of the verbs in the present perfect tense. Then identify the infinitive form of each verb. The first one is done for you.

☞ REVIEW SCHRITT 8: The present perfect tense

NIELS: <u>Hast</u> du <u>gehört</u>?	hören
Sara ist letzte Woche in eine neue Wohnung eingezogen.	1. _____
SONJA: Tatsächlich! Das habe ich nicht gewusst.	2. _____
Bisher (*until now*) haben wir alle im Studentenwohnheim gewohnt.	3. _____
Wie hat sie die neue Wohnung gefunden?	4. _____
NIELS: Sie hat eine Anzeige (*ad*) in der Zeitung gelesen.	5. _____
SONJA: Hast du die Wohnung schon gesehen?	6. _____
NIELS: Ja. Gestern bin ich mit Markus zu ihr gegangen und	7. _____
wir haben uns die Wohnung angesehen.	8. _____
Ihre neue Mitbewohnerin ist um 18.00 nach Hause gekommen	9. _____
und wir haben alle zusammen gekocht.	10. _____

SONJA: Wie lange seid ihr da geblieben?

NIELS: Nicht sehr spät. Saras Mitbewohnerin ist krank geworden.

Sie hat zwei Aspirin genommen

und hat schon um 20.30 Uhr geschlafen.

11. _____

12. _____

13. _____

14. _____

5-9 Letztes Wochenende. Sara tells about her weekend with her parents. Complete the paragraph with the appropriate past participles from the list. (*Hint:* The auxiliary verb should help you narrow the list of possible participles that can be used in each sentence.)

☞ REVIEW SCHRITT 8: The present perfect tense

aufgeräumt	gefahren	geputzt	gesehen
ausgegangen	gegangen	geregnet	gewesen
besucht	gegessen	gesaugt	
geblieben	gekommen	geschmeckt	

Am Wochenende haben mich meine Eltern in meiner neuen Wohnung

(1) _____. Am Freitagabend habe ich also mein Zimmer

(2) _____ und das Bad (3) _____. Meine Mitbewohnerin

hat Staub (4) _____. Dann sind wir früh ins Bett (5) _____.

Meine Eltern sind am Samstagmorgen um 9.00 Uhr (6) _____. Das Wetter

ist nicht schön (7) _____ — es hat (8) _____. Wir sind fast

den ganzen Tag zu Hause (9) _____. Am Abend sind wir aber

(10) _____. Wir haben einen interessanten Film (11) _____,

und nachher haben wir in einem tollen chinesischen Restaurant

(12) _____. Alles hat uns sehr gut (13) _____. Um 21.00 Uhr

sind meine Eltern wieder nach Hause (14) _____. Es war ein schöner

Besuch.

5-10 Das letzte Mal. Choose ten activities from the list below and indicate when you last did each of the following activities. Use phrases like **gestern, letzten Monat, am Montag**, and so on, or **noch nie** if you have never done a particular activity. Use the present perfect tense.

☞ REVIEW SCHRITT 8: The present perfect tense

10 Kilometer joggen	bis (*until*) 14.00 Uhr schlafen
Deutsch sprechen	ein Auto mieten
im Garten arbeiten	E-Mails schreiben
Freunde fotografieren	Hausaufgaben machen
in der Bibliothek lernen	in der Dusche singen
Kaffee trinken	Karten spielen
meinen Großeltern helfen	Motorrad fahren
Schlittschuh laufen	zum Supermarkt gehen
	?

BEISPIEL: Wäsche waschen
→ Ich habe gestern Wäsche gewaschen.
nach Europa reisen
→ Ich bin noch nie nach Europa gereist.

1. _____

2. _____

3. _____

4. _____

5. _____

6. _____

7. _____

8. _____

9. _____

10. _____

5-11 Meine Kindheit. How often did you do each of these activities as a child: **immer**, **oft**, **manchmal**, **selten**, or **nie**? Use the present perfect tense.

☞ REVIEW SCHRITT 10: Separable and inseparable prefix verbs

BEISPIEL: meine Spielzeuge (*toys*) kaputtmachen
→ Ich habe meine Spielzeuge selten kaputtgemacht.

1. gute Noten (*grades*) bekommen

_____

2. einkaufen

_____

3. fernsehen

_____

4. Freunde anrufen

_____

5. Freunde besuchen

_____

6. früh aufstehen

_____

7. mein Zimmer aufräumen

_____

8. meine Eltern verstehen

_____

9. mit Freunden ausgehen

_____

10. Witze erzählen

_____

5-12 Gute Vorsätze. You decide to get your life in order. Which of the following things will you do and which will you not do in the coming month? Use the present tense.

☞ REVIEW SCHRITT 10: Separable and inseparable prefix verbs

aus dem Studentenwohnheim ausziehen	den Fußboden aufwischen
Familie und Freunde einladen	mein Zimmer neu einrichten
meine Bücher verkaufen	meine Eltern anrufen
meine Kreditkarte benutzen	meine Großeltern / einen Freund / ? besuchen
meine Wohnung aufräumen	in eine neue Wohnung einziehen
Miete bezahlen	viel Geld verdienen
viel fernsehen	. . .

BEISPIEL: Ich benutze meine Kreditkarte nicht.
Ich richte mein Zimmer neu ein.

1. _____

2. _____

3. _____

4. _____

5. _____

6. _____

7. _____

8. _____

Alles klar?

5-13 Letztes Wochenende. Write what you did last weekend. Write at least eight sentences. Use the present perfect tense.

_____

_____

_____

_____

_____

_____

_____

_____

5-14 Die Familie Gladbach. Read the passage below about Elke and Veit Gladbach's living situation and see how much information you can glean from the text on your first reading. Remember that you do not need to understand every word to get the gist of a text. Then read the text a second time and search specifically for the answers to the questions that follow. Answer them in complete sentences.

Veit und Elke Gladbach wohnen in Bielefeld. Sie möchten ein Haus kaufen, aber Häuser sind in Deutschland sehr teuer. Vor vier Jahren sind Veit und Elke in eine Dreizimmerwohnung eingezogen und haben sie sehr schön eingerichtet. Sie haben neue Geschirrschränke in die Küche eingebaut und haben auch einen Herd, einen Kühlschrank und einen Geschirrspüler gekauft. Alle Wände haben sie auch mit frischen, neuen Farben gestrichen. Außer Bad und Küche haben sie ein Schlafzimmer und ein Wohnzimmer. Sie haben auch ein Arbeitszimmer gehabt, aber letztes Jahr haben sie aus dem Arbeitszimmer ein Kinderzimmer gemacht, denn Elke hat im April ein Kind bekommen. Die Wohnung gefällt ihnen gut. Sie haben keinen Garten, aber es gibt einen Balkon, und da haben sie im Frühjahr und im Sommer viele Blumen und Pflanzen.

Elke ist Lehrerin gewesen, aber jetzt bleibt sie zu Hause mit ihrem Sohn. Die Familie verdient jetzt weniger Geld, aber sie bekommen auch Kindergeld und das hilft. Vor ein paar Monaten war Elke bei ihrer Ärztin und hat erfahren (*found out*), sie bekommt bald ein zweites Kind. Das Ehepaar ist sehr glücklich. Sie meinen aber, die Wohnung wird bald zu klein. Eine Vierzimmerwohnung ist ihnen zu teuer, aber wo soll das zweite Kind schlafen? Was passiert, wenn die Kinder älter werden? Elke und Veit müssen sich bald entscheiden (*decide*), was sie machen wollen.

1. Wo wohnen Veit und Elke Gladbach?

_____

2. Warum kaufen sie kein Haus?

_____

3. Wie haben sie ihre Wohnung eingerichtet?

_____

4. Warum haben sie kein Arbeitszimmer?

_____

5. Warum arbeitet Elke nicht mehr als Lehrerin?

_____

6. Was hat Elkes Ärztin ihr gesagt?

_____

7. Soll die Familie ausziehen und eine neue Wohnung suchen? Warum (nicht)? Was soll die Familie Gladbach in dieser Situation machen?

_____

_____

_____

_____

_____

5-15 Mein Traumhaus. If you could live wherever and however you wanted, how would your dream home be? What would it absolutely have to have and what would not be part of your dream house? What should it look like? Where should it be located? Describe your dream home. Write a paragraph of at least eight sentences.

BEISPIEL: Mein Traumhaus soll . . .   Ich möchte . . .
Es muss . . . haben.   Es darf nicht . . . sein.

_____

_____

_____

_____

_____

_____

_____

_____

_____

_____

Kultur

5-16 Kulturnotizen. Briefly answer the following questions in English based on the **Kulturnotizen** sections of **Kapitel 5**.

. What are **Schrebergärten**, and why are they popular in Germany? How do they differ from gardens in North America?

_____

_____

_____

_____

_____

_____

_____

_____

2. Why do the majority of people in German-speaking countries rent apartments rather than owning their own homes? How is the situation similar to or different from where you live?

_____

_____

_____

_____

_____

_____

_____

_____

3. In what ways do Germans use their living space differently than you? Why do you think these differences exist?

_____

_____

_____

_____

_____

_____

_____

_____

4. What role do the German-speaking countries play in the European Union?

_____

_____

_____

_____

_____

_____

_____

_____

5-17 Die Europäische Union. Outline the area of the map that represents the current membership of the EU. Then label **in German** all the German-speaking countries and those that border them. Consult the maps on the inside cover of *Alles klar?*, if necessary.

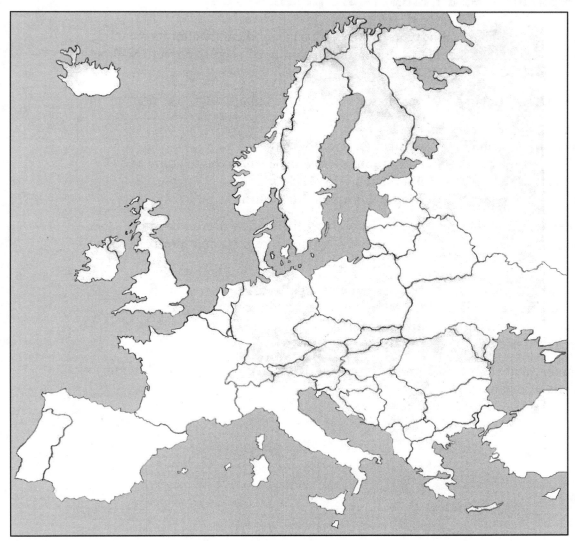

5-18 EU-Schnitzeljagd (*scavenger hunt*). Briefly answer the following questions about the European Union. How many of the answers can you find?

1. How many countries are currently members of the EU?   _____

2. Which member nation has the highest population?   _____

3. Which member has the biggest land area?   _____

4. Which EU candidate (or member nation) lies partly in Asia?   _____

5. Name 2 Western European nations that are not EU members.   _____

6. Which is larger: the EU population or the US population?   _____

Erweiterung

More on separable and inseparable prefix verbs

You have probably noticed that adding a prefix to a verb can significantly alter its meaning; however, sometimes you will be able to predict the meaning of a prefixed verb without having to look it up.

You will notice that the English equivalents of verbs with prefixes often use prefixes of their own:

beschreiben = to *de*scribe   **entdecken** = to *dis*cover
vor•schreiben = to *pre*scribe   **entkommen** = to *escape* (*literally:* to come away)
verstehen = to *under*stand   **übersehen** = to *over*look
verschlafen = to *over*sleep   **wieder•kommen** = to *re*turn

Alternatively, the English equivalents of verbs with prefixes often use a verb plus other modifying words, such as prepositions or adverbs—much like separable prefix verbs in German:

aus•gehen = to go out   **zurück•geben** = to give back
zu•hören = to listen to   **wieder•sehen** = to see / meet again
heraus•finden = to find out   **auf•schreiben** = to write down
verbrauchen = to use up   **bezahlen** = to pay for

The more separable and inseparable prefix verbs you learn, the more you will begin to recognize patterns of meaning.

6-9 Was ist los? Monika's friends are having a difficult weekend. What aches and pains do they have, based on the descriptions of their activities?

☞ REVIEW SCHRITT 6: Aua! Es tut mir hier weh!

BEISPIEL: Karl-Heinz hat den ganzen Tag im Garten gearbeitet.
→ Der Rücken tut ihm weh.

1. Konrad war gestern Abend auf einer Party und hat zu viel Bier getrunken.

   _____

2. Elvira ist beim Radfahren hingefallen (*fell*).

   _____

3. Hilda ist heute in einem großen Marathon gelaufen.

   _____

4. Reinhard hat heute in der Bibliothek drei Bücher gelesen.

   _____

5. Angelika hat heute drei lange Examen geschrieben.

   _____

6. Theodor und Werner sind heute in ihre neue Wohnung eingezogen. Sie haben ihre Möbel und viele Kartons getragen (*carried*).

   _____

7. Adam hat Kaffee getrunken und der Kaffee war zu heiß.

   _____

6-10 Teenager. Monika's younger siblings still live at home. Complete the dialogue with the correct accusative or dative reflexive pronouns.

☞ REVIEW SCHRITT 8: Reflexive verbs

FRAU SCHRÖDER: Kommt ihr? Ihr müsst (1) _____ fertig machen. Ihr müsst doch in wenigen Minuten zur Schule.

(*Luise und Albert kommen in die Küche.*)

FRAU SCHRÖDER: Was soll das denn, Luise? Das trägst (*wear*) du nicht zur Schule! Du

gehst sofort zurück zu deinem Zimmer und ziehst (2) _____

um. Und du kannst (3) _____ auch das Gesicht waschen. Du bist viel zu jung für so viel Schminke.

LUISE: Nein, ich ziehe (4) _____ nicht um. Ich mag dieses T-Shirt

und diese Jeans. Und das Gesicht wasche ich (5) _____ auch nicht.

FRAU SCHRÖDER: So was von frech (*cheeky*)! Und was soll das, Albert? Rasierst du

(6) _____ gar nicht mehr?

ALBERT: Warum regst du (7) _____ so auf? Das sind doch unsere Körper.

FRAU SCHRÖDER: Was ist los mit unseren Kindern, Helmut? Siehst du das nicht? Der eine (*One*) will (8) _____ nicht rasieren, die andere (*the other*) schminkt (9) _____ zu sehr.

HERR SCHRÖDER: Ach, Inge, sie sind eben Teenager.

FRAU SCHRÖDER: Ich mache (10) _____ wirklich Sorgen um die Kinder, Helmut. Was soll aus ihnen werden?

HERR SCHRÖDER: Regen wir (11) _____ nicht auf, in fünf Jahren werden sie wieder normale Menschen.

6-11 Was Susi noch tun muss. Frau Schröder still has to get her youngest daughter ready for school. What does she tell little Susi to do?

☞ REVIEW SCHRITT 8: Reflexive verbs

BEISPIEL: Susi trägt noch ihren Schlafanzug (*pajamas*).
→ Maria: "Susi, du musst dich noch anziehen."

1. Susi muss unter die Dusche gehen.

   FRAU SCHRÖDER: "_____"
2. Susis Haare sind noch schmutzig.

   FRAU SCHRÖDER: "_____"
3. Susi ist nach der Dusche ganz nass (*wet*).

   FRAU SCHRÖDER: "_____"
4. Susis Haare sind ungepflegt (*unkempt*).

   FRAU SCHRÖDER: "_____"
5. Susi hat gerade gefrühstückt.

   FRAU SCHRÖDER: "_____"
6. Susis Schule fängt um 9.00 Uhr an. Es ist jetzt 8.45 Uhr.

   FRAU SCHRÖDER: "_____"

6-15 Was Österreicher für ihre Gesundheit tun. Order the health and fitness activities of Austrians in 2002 from the most to the least frequent (1-11).

_____ öfter zum Arzt gehen   _____ Wellness-Urlaube machen

_____ alternative Medizin probieren   _____ sich gesund ernähren

_____ Sport treiben   _____ Kilos abnehmen (*take off*)

_____ laufen, spazieren, wandern   _____ regelmäßig zur Vorsorgeuntersuchung gehen

_____ sich in Gesundheitsfragen   _____ asiatische Gesundheitsübungen ausprobieren
informieren

_____ Vitamintabletten nehmen

6-16 Ihre Gesundheit. What do you do for your health? What else should you do? Write at least six sentences.

_____

_____

_____

_____

_____

_____

_____

_____

Kultur

6-17 Kulturnotizen. Briefly answer the following questions in English based on the **Kulturnotizen** sections of **Kapitel 6**.

1. What do Germans typically do during a **Kur**? Have you ever done something similar?

_____

_____

_____

_____

_____

_____

_____

_____

2. What are the similarities and differences between the German health care system and that of your own country?

_____

_____

_____

_____

_____

_____

_____

_____

3. What is the intent of and what are some of the provisions of the German "social state"? How does this compare to where you live?

_____

_____

_____

_____

_____

_____

_____

_____

4. Compare German dating practices and attitudes about the body with those of your own culture.

_____

_____

_____

_____

_____

_____

_____

_____

Erweiterung

The verb *lassen*

The German **lassen** is a commonly used verb that has a variety of uses. It is used like a modal verb, in that it is usually accompanied by a second verb, which appears in its infinitive form at the end of a sentence. It is this second verb that often determines the exact meaning of **lassen**.

In its most basic and literal usage, **lassen** means *to leave* (*something somewhere*). In this sense, it can be used either with or without another verb.

> Er **lässt** seinen Hund zu Hause.
> *He is leaving his dog at home.*

> Wir **lassen** unsere Sachen auf dem Tisch **liegen**.
> *We are leaving our things lying on the table.*

It can also mean *to let* or *to permit* something:

> **Lasst** ihr die Kinder **spielen**?
> *Are you letting the children play?*

> Ich **lasse** dich das Auto **fahren**.
> *I'll let you drive the car.*

The verb **lassen** also means *to have* or *get something done*. With this meaning, a reflexive pronoun is often used:

> Ich **lasse mir** die Haare **schneiden**.
> *I am getting my hair cut.*

> Meine Eltern **lassen sich** zum Flughafen **fahren**.
> *My parents are having someone drive them to the airport.*
> (*My parents are having themselves driven to the airport.*)

When **lassen** is used reflexively, it can also mean *to be able to be* or *can be*. In this case, it is always used with another verb.

> Das Fenster **lässt sich** nicht **öffnen**.
> *The window cannot be opened.*

> Das Buch **lässt sich lesen**.
> *The book makes for good reading.* (*The book is readable.*)

Note that **lassen** has a present tense stem change (**a → ä**)

6-18 Es lässt sich übersetzen. Translate the following sentences into Englilsh, paying particular attention to the meaning of the verb **lassen.**

1. Meine Mutter lässt das Haus putzen.

   _____

2. Manchmal lassen Studenten ihre Hausaufgaben zu Hause.

   _____

3. Die Professorin lässt die Studenten nach Hause gehen.

   _____

4. Wir lassen uns die Adressen geben.

   _____

5. Ich lasse mir den Witz erklären.

   _____

6. Mein Vater lässt seinen BMW in der Garage.

   _____

7. Das Auto lässt sich fahren.

   _____

8. Lasst ihr mich schlafen?

   _____

6-19 In Luxus leben. You just inherited millions and can now afford to live in the lap of luxury. Think of things you will no longer do yourself. Bearing in mind that money is no object, list at least four things you will now have others do for you.

BEISPIEL: Ich lasse mir jeden Tag das Abendessen kochen.
                  Ich lasse mir die Füße waschen.

1. _____

2. _____

3. _____

4. _____

Lass uns etwas zusammen unternehmen!

Themenwortschatz

7-1 Wortsuche: In der Stadt. You go to the city on a shopping trip and buy the following things, each in a different place. Find the hidden names of the places in the grid!

Aspirin	ein Buch	Rosen
Bratwurst	Butter	Seife
Briefmarken	eine Fahrkarte	Socken
Brot	einen Kaffee	

W	E	I	P	R	B	U	C	H	H	A	N	D	L	U	N	G	B	R	I
A	S	C	A	F	É	L	B	Ö	T	H	A	Z	R	M	N	D	K	L	S
Q	C	H	O	K	A	U	F	H	A	U	S	P	R	I	Z	O	J	G	M
R	H	Ä	M	X	H	V	L	K	D	R	B	A	H	N	H	O	F	Ö	E
L	E	B	E	N	S	M	I	T	T	E	L	G	E	S	C	H	Ä	F	T
T	P	Ö	N	I	Z	A	O	D	B	G	U	F	K	N	E	I	L	D	Z
A	B	N	A	H	E	K	X	R	Ä	Y	M	O	B	S	O	Y	M	I	G
U	Ä	D	D	L	Y	B	Y	O	C	H	E	N	G	U	S	P	I	L	E
P	C	M	S	Z	G	A	J	G	X	W	N	Ü	M	N	T	H	R	K	R
P	K	S	M	P	D	X	D	E	W	E	L	V	P	Y	N	G	Q	J	E
M	E	O	A	O	B	C	I	R	Å	X	A	P	O	T	H	E	K	E	I
Y	R	P	Å	S	H	G	T	I	S	G	D	Q	F	Ö	P	R	Ü	Z	E
O	E	U	S	T	B	U	C	E	V	Q	E	S	D	U	S	K	E	R	Z
W	I	L	K	R	E	I	D	S	K	Ü	N	L	P	R	M	A	U	D	R

7-2 Urlaub in Deutschland. Pietro and Giovanni live in Italy but are spending their vacation in Germany. Complete the description of the first day of their vacation with the correct forms (cases, verb inflections) of the following words.

der Bahnhof	der Fluss	ein Restaurant
die Bushaltestelle	herauskommen	ein Stadtplan
einsteigen	hineingehen	stehen
die Fahrkarten	eine Kneipe	der Zug

Pietro und Giovanni wohnen in Florenz und möchten nach Köln fahren. Sie haben kein Auto, also möchten sie mit (1) _____ fahren. Sie gehen zu (2) _____, kaufen (3) _____ und (4) _____ in den Zug _____. Nach 8 Stunden sind sie in Köln. Sie (5) _____ aus dem Bahnhof _____ und sehen sofort den Kölner Dom, denn er (6) _____ direkt vor dem Bahnhof.

Sie kennen Köln nicht so gut, aber Giovanni hat (7) _____. Sie möchten zum Hotel fahren und warten an (8) _____ auf den Bus. Das Hotel liegt am Rhein. Pietro und Giovanni lassen ihre Rucksäcke im Hotel und gehen (9) _____ entlang zurück in die Stadt. Sie wollen etwas essen und finden (10) _____. Sie (11) _____, und setzen sich. Nach dem Essen trinken sie in (12) _____ ein Bier. Dann gehen sie zum Hotel zurück und schlafen. Der erste Tag ihres Urlaubs ist schließlich (*after all*) schon ein langer Tag gewesen!

Schritte

7-3 Wo machen Sie das? Indicate where you do the following activities.

☞ REVIEW SCHRITT 1: In der Stadt
          SCHRITT 2: Destination versus location: Two-way prepositions

BEISPIEL: Ihr Auto parken   → Ich parke mein Auto im Parkhaus.
          ODER   → Ich parke mein Auto in der Garage.

1. kochen   _____

2. tanzen   _____

3. einen Film sehen   _____

4. schlafen   _____

5. essen   _____

6. Hausaufgaben machen   _____

7. fernsehen   _____

8. sich die Haare waschen   _____

9. singen   _____

7-4 Wohin gehört das? You had a party at your place last night and some friends stayed over to help you clean up. However, they're not sure where things belong. Tell them where to put the items.

☞ REVIEW SCHRITT 2: Destination versus location: Two-way prepositions

BEISPIEL: Wohin gehört das schmutzige Geschirr?   →   in den Geschirrspüler
                                        ODER   neben das Spülbecken

1. Wohin gehören die Weingläser?   _____

2. Wohin gehören die CDs?   _____

3. Wohin gehört das Fotoalbum?   _____

4. Wohin gehört die Milch?   _____

5. Wohin gehören die Videokassetten?   _____

6. Wohin gehört der Müll?   _____

7. Wohin gehören die Stühle?   _____

8. Wohin gehören die schmutzigen Handtücher? _____

7-5 Vor der Party. It's Saturday morning and Horst and Antje are getting ready for a party at their house. Complete the dialogue with the correct accusative ordative definite articles.

☞ REVIEW SCHRITT 2: Destination versus location: Two-way prepositions

HORST: Komm, Antje! Wir haben heute noch viel zu tun.

ANTJE: Ja, ich weiß. Wollen wir in (1) _____ Stadt fahren?

HORST: Wie bitte? Schau unsere Wohnung doch mal an — wir müssen aufräumen! Die Wäsche liegt auf (2) _____ Sofa, deine Bücher sind auf (3) _____ Esstisch, und viele alte Zeitungen liegen auf (4) _____ Boden.

ANTJE: Wo sollen wir beginnen? Kannst du die Wäsche in (5) _____ Schrank tun? Ich bringe die Zeitungen in (6) _____ Garage und stelle die Bücher in (7) _____ Bücherregal.

HORST: Ja, gut. Ich tue das schmutzige Geschirr in (8) _____ Geschirrspüler. Wir müssen auch noch in (9) _____ Wohnzimmer Staub saugen. Steht der Staubsauger noch in (10) _____ Garage zwischen (11) _____ Mülleimern?

ANTJE: Ich weiß nicht. Vor ein paar Wochen war er in (12) _____ Ecke neben (13) _____ Besen.

HORST: In (14) _____ Küche müssen wir den Boden auch noch aufwischen.

ANTJE: Wir müssen vor (15) _____ Party wirklich noch viel tun.

HORST: Ach, schau mal! Meine Armbanduhr war unter (16) _____ Zeitungen. Wir müssen wirklich öfter aufräumen, Antje.

7-6 Wie komme ich dahin? You are in Josefstadt at the **Tourist-Information** and have received directions to various locations in the city. Which directions take you where?

☞ REVIEW SCHRITT 5: Die Stadt kennen lernen

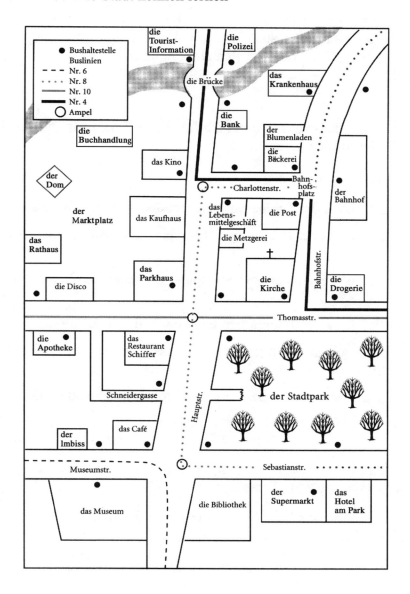

1. Gehen Sie über die Brücke immer geradeaus. An der zweiten Ampel gehen Sie nach links. Gehen Sie an der Kirche vorbei und da an der Ecke gegenüber vom Stadtpark sehen Sie _____.

2. Gehen Sie über die Brücke immer geradeaus. Gehen Sie am Kino vorbei, dann in die Charlottenstraße gleich links. Gehen Sie die Straße entlang bis kurz vor dem Bahnhof. Da sehen Sie gleich links die Bäckerei und an der Ecke direkt gegenüber von der Bäckerei steht _____.

3. Gehen Sie über den Fluss und an der Bank vorbei. Rechts sehen Sie das Kino. Gehen Sie da rechts zwischen dem Kino und dem Kaufhaus in die Fußgängerzone hinein. Gehen Sie rechts über den Marktplatz und da neben dem Dom sehen Sie

   _____.

4. Steigen Sie hier in die Nummer 4 ein. Fahren Sie bis zum Kino und da steigen Sie um. Fahren Sie mit der Nummer 8 an dem Stadtpark vorbei. Der Bus biegt in die Sebastianstraße links ab. Steigen Sie an der nächsten Haltestelle aus. Da ist

   _____.

7-7 Wo ist das? You are studying the map of Josefstadt (above in **7-6**), trying to orient yourself. What do you find in the following locations?

☞ REVIEW SCHRITT 5: Die Stadt kennen lernen

1. _____ ist in der Thomasstraße gegenüber von der Disco.

2. _____ ist an der Kreuzung Charlottenstraße und Hauptstraße neben der Metzgerei.

3. _____ ist gegenüber vom Stadtpark, zwischen dem Hotel und der Bibliothek.

4. _____ ist in der Bahnhofstraße in der Nähe vom Fluss.

5. _____ steht an der Kreuzung Thomasstraße und Bahnhofstraße gegenüber von der Drogerie.

6. _____ findet man in der Fußgängerzone zwischen dem Dom und der Disco.

7-8 Ihre Stadt. Describe where things are in your city—either your hometown or your university town. You do not need to use complete sentences.

☞ REVIEW SCHRITT 2: Destination versus location: Two-way prepositions
        SCHRITT 5: Die Stadt kennen lernen

BEISPIEL: Wo ist das Museum? → in der Maximilianstraße neben der Post

1. Wo ist Ihre Bank? _____

2. Wo ist ein Kino? _____

3. Wo ist die Unibibliothek? _____

4. Wo ist das Rathaus? _____

5. Wo ist ein Park? _____

6. Wo ist Ihre Wohnung? _____

Alles klar?

7-13 Ihre Wohnung. Think of at least six objects in your room or apartment and state where each is located. Use as many of the two-way prepositions as you can. Remember: Two-way prepositions use the dative case to indicate locations.

BEISPIEL: Mein Schreibtisch steht in der Ecke neben dem Bett.
Meine Mikrowelle ist in der Küche über dem Herd.

1. _____
2. _____
3. _____
4. _____
5. _____
6. _____

7-14 Ihre neue Wohnung. It's moving day, and you just finished transporting all of your things to your new apartment. Where are you going to put everything? Remember: two-way prepositions use the accusative case to indicate destinations.

BEISPIEL: Ich stelle das Bett ins Schlafzimmer unter das Fenster.
Ich lege meinen Teddybären auf das Bett zwischen die Kopfkissen.

1. _____
2. _____
3. _____
4. _____
5. _____
6. _____

7-15 Situationen. How would you respond in the following situations?

1. You are in Hamburg and have lost your bearings. You're looking for the train station. You stop a stranger on the street and say:

   _____

2. You're having a barbecue at your place on Saturday and the German exchange student you invited needs directions from the university to your room / apartment. You tell him:

_____

_____

_____

_____

_____

3. A German tourist stops you on the street near your university and asks you how to get to the nearest train or bus station. You tell her:

_____

_____

_____

_____

_____

7-16 In der Großstadt. Read the following passage about Klaus's life and routine and complete the prepositional phrases with the correct articles, based on the given cues. Pay special attention to case endings.

Klaus kommt **aus** (1) _____ (*a*) kleinen Stadt in Norddeutschland, aber

jetzt wohnt er **in** (2) _____ (*the*) Großstadt Hamburg. Er wohnt schon **seit**

(3) _____ (*a*) Jahr da, und die Wohngegend gefällt ihm sehr. Seine Wohnung

ist klein, aber alles ist in der Nähe. Das Wohnhaus steht **zwischen** (4) _____

(*a*) Bäckerei und (5) _____ (*a*) Café, und ein Supermarkt ist gleich **um**

(6) _____ (*the*) Ecke.

Er arbeitet **für** (7) _____ (*the*) Stadt und hat ein Büro **in** (8) _____

(*the*) Rathaus. Er hat nichts **gegen** (9) _____ (*this*) Arbeit; eigentlich gefällt

sie ihm gut. Fast jeden Tag fährt er **mit** (10) _____ (*the*) U-Bahn **zu**

(11) _____ (*the*) Rathaus, denn die U-Bahnhaltestelle ist direkt gegenüber **von**

(12) _____ (*his*) Wohnung.

Freitagabends trifft er seine Freundin oft **nach** (13) _____ (*the*) Arbeit **in**

(14) _____ (*a*) netten Restaurant, und danach gehen sie zusammen **in**

(15) _____ (*a*) Kneipe oder **in** (16) _____ (*the*) Disco. Klaus findet

das Leben in der Großstadt einfach toll.

Lesestück: Hamburg ist nicht nur für Hamburger

Why does Klaus like living in Hamburg? Read the text below, scanning for information that might explain why a person would want to live in Hamburg. As you find information that you think answers this question, underline it. Remember that you do not need to understand every single word to glean important information from the text.

Hansestadt Hamburg

Die Stadt Hamburg ist das wirtschaftliche[1] und kulturelle Zentrum von Norddeutschland. Mit 1,7 Millionen Einwohnern ist sie die zweitgrößte Stadt Deutschlands und ist zugleich auch eins von den 16 Bundesländern der Bundesrepublik Deutschland. Diese Metropole des Nordens ist also — wie Bremen und Berlin — ein Stadtstaat.

Das Leben am Wasser bestimmt diese Stadt wie keine andere Metropole. Hamburg liegt an einem Fluss, der Elbe. Mitten im Herzen der Stadt liegt auch ein großer See: die Alster. Kanäle und Wasserwege und -flächen nehmen 8 Prozent des Stadtgebiets ein. Die Stadt hat 2302 Brücken — mehr als Venedig und Amsterdam zusammen! See und Fluss sind gut nicht nur für Wassersport, Spaziergänge und Boottouren. Die Stadt ist schon seit dem Mittelalter ein sehr wichtiger Nordseehafen.[2] Er steht heute im Mittelpunkt des Handels[3] mit Ost- und Nordeuropa. Als Containerhafen nimmt er den zweiten Platz in Europa und den siebten Platz in der Welt ein.

Ihre wirtschaftliche Stärke verdankt die Stadt aber nicht nur ihrem Hafen. Hamburg ist auch eins der größten Zentren der deutschen Medienwirtschaft[4]. Mehr als 50 Prozent aller deutschen Zeitungen und Zeitschriften[5] kommen aus Hamburg und über 50.000 Einwohner arbeiten im Medienbereich. Die Stadt ist ebenfalls ein Standort hochspezialisierter Industrien wie Medizin- und Biotechnik und Flugzeugbau. Und wer auf einem Steinway-Klavier spielt, sich mit Nivea-Hautcreme einreibt oder mit einem Montblanc-Stift schreibt, benutzt Hamburger Produkte.

Wegen seiner Lage am Wasser und seiner starken Wirtschaft aber auch aus anderen Gründen, bietet Hamburg eine hohe Lebensqualität. Mit 30 Quadratmetern Wohnfläche[6] pro Person hat Hamburg die größte durchschnittliche Wohnfläche aller Großstädte der Welt. Trotz der Großstadtatmosphäre machen auch Parks und Grünflächen 14 Prozent des Stadtgebiets aus. Zudem ist das kulturelle Angebot Hamburgs genauso vielfältig wie seine Wirtschaft. Hamburg hat zwei Staatstheater und die Hamburgische Staatsoper ist weltbekannt. Es gibt zudem über 30 private Theater, 50 staatliche und private Museen, 30 Kinos und rund 4000 Restaurants.

Die 1200 Jahre alte Stadt hat also ein vielseitiges Gesicht. Rund um die Alster leben die Menschen gut.

[1] economic   [2] North Sea harbor   [3] trade
[4] media market   [5] periodicals   [6] living space area

7-17 Hamburg in Zahlen. Complete each of the following statements with a number based on the information in the text above.

1. Hamburg hat _____ Einwohner.

2. Pro Person hat Hamburg _____ Quadratmeter Wohnfläche.

3. _____ Prozent der Stadt besteht aus Wasser.

4. _____ Prozent der Stadt besteht aus Parks und Grünanlagen.

5. _____ Prozent aller deutschen Zeitungen und Zeitschriften
   kommen aus Hamburg.

6. Die Stadt ist _____ Jahre alt.

7. Die Stadt hat _____ Brücken.

8. Hamburg hat _____ Staatstheater, _____
   private Theater und _____ Museen.

9. _____ Hamburger arbeiten in den Medien.

7-18 In Hamburg wohnen. Would you like to live in Hamburg? Write a short paragraph of at least six sentences explaining why or why not. Use information from the text to support your response. You might like to start your paragraph with: **Ich möchte (nicht) gern in Hamburg wohnen, denn . . .**

_____

_____

_____

_____

_____

_____

_____

Kultur

7-19 Kulturnotizen. Briefly answer the following questions in English based on the **Kulturnotizen** sections of **Kapitel 7**.

1. Does your hometown or university town have an **Altstadt**? How does the layout of your city compare to that of a German city? What are the similarities and differences? What are the reasons for the differences?

_____

_____

_____

_____

_____

_____

_____

2. What differences are there between libraries in Europe and the United States? Have you ever been to an especially interesting library?

_____

_____

_____

_____

_____

_____

_____

3. How does the system of local public transportation in Germany, Austria, and Switzerland compare with the public transport system in your hometown? In your university town?

_____

_____

_____

_____

_____

_____

_____

4. What German holiday traditions are similar to those of your family? Which German holidays are not typically celebrated in your country?

_____

_____

_____

_____

_____

_____

_____

Erweiterung

Prepositions meaning *to*

You may have noticed that German has several different prepositions that correspond to the English word *to*. You learned two of these prepositions in **Kapitel 5**, namely, the dative prepositions **nach** and **zu**. The two-way prepositions **in** and **auf**, which you learned in this chapter, can also mean *to* when used with the accusative case. Examine the following distinctions:

nach	with the names of most cities, countries, continents, and so on. **nach Baltimore** (*to Baltimore*), **nach Japan** (*to Japan*), **nach Afrika** (*to Africa*) also: **nach Hause** (*to / in the direction of home*)
zu	with people, places of business indicated by a person's profession, and names of businesses **zu Veronika** (*to Veronika's house*), **zu meinen Eltern** (*to my parents' house*), **zum Arzt** (*to the doctor*), **zum Bäcker** (*to the baker's*), **zu Ikea** (*to Ikea*) with locales that are temporary transfer points **zum Bahnhof** (*to the train station*), **zum Flughafen** (*to the airport*), **zur Bushaltestelle** (*to the bus stop*) with certain public buildings or institutions[1] **zur Bank** (*to the bank*), **zur Post** (*to the post office*), **zum Rathaus** (*to city hall*), **zur Polizei** (*to the police*), **zur Universität** (*to the university*) with spectator sports events **zum Fußballspiel** (*to the soccer game*), **zu den Olympischen Spielen** (*to the Olympic games*)
in	with the names of countries that have a feminine or plural article **in die Schweiz** (*to Switzerland*), **in die Niederlande** (*to the Netherlands*) with enclosed spaces such as buildings[2] **ins Krankenhaus** (*to the hospital*), **in die Bäckerei** (*to the bakery*), **in die Kirche** (*to church*) with events that occur in enclosed spaces **ins Theater** (*to the theater*), **ins Konzert** (*to a concert*), **in die Oper** (*to the opera*)
auf	with open spaces **auf den Markt** (*to the market*), **auf das Land** (*to the country*), **auf den Spielplatz** (*to the playground*)

[1] With these public buildings, **auf** is often used as an alternative: **auf die Bank, auf die Post, aufs Rathaus, auf die Polizei, auf die Universität.**

[2] In general, one uses **in** rather than **zu** with destinations where one intends to spend a reasonably long time. **Zu** suggests a more superficial visit. Compare the following sentences: **Michael geht in die Bibliothek** implies that Michael is going to the library to do some research or to study. He will stay there for a while to accomplish some task. **Micheal geht zur Bibliothek** suggests that he is headed for the library, but it is not clear whether he will stay there long; maybe he's just dropping off a book. Whereas the first sentence conveys that the library is a purposeful destination and suggests that Michael will be engaged in some meaningful, extended activity after his arrival there, the second sentence places more emphasis on his movement in the direction of the library.

7-20 Wohin? Complete the paragraph with the proper prepositions. Include the definite article, where necessary.

Dorothea studiert in Augsburg und ist am Wochenende mit dem Zug (1) _____ München gefahren. Sie ist (2) _____ ihrer Freundin Charlotte gefahren, denn sie hatten sich seit langer Zeit nicht gesehen. Am Freitagabend sind sie zuerst (3) _____ Restaurant und dann (4) _____ Disco gegangen. Sie haben die ganze Nacht durch getanzt. Sie sind am Samstag (5) _____ den Markt gegangen und haben da eingekauft. Später sind sie (6) _____ Kino gegangen und haben den neuen Film von Steven Spielberg gesehen. Danach sind sie wieder (7) _____ Hause gegangen und haben gekocht. Am Sonntag sind sie durch die Stadt spazieren gegangen. Sie sind (8) _____ Park gegangen und haben dort ein Picknick gemacht. Am Abend ist Charlotte mit Dorothea (9) _____ Bahnhof gegangen. Der Besuch hat ihnen sehr viel Spaß gemacht.

Kapitel 8

Ja gerne, aber . . .

Themenwortschatz

8-1 Was tragen Sie? Name two or three items of clothing or accessories you wear in each of the following situations. Remember to include the correct article and adjective endings, where appropriate.

BEISPIEL: am Strand → eine Sonnenbrille, Sandalen, mein dunkelgrüner Bikini

1. an der Universität

   _____

2. im Schwimmbad

   _____

3. in einem teuren Restaurant

   _____

4. auf einer Skireise

   _____

5. bei einer Wanderung

   _____

6. samstagmorgens zu Hause

   _____

7. auf einer Hochzeit

   _____

8-2 Laura und Nadia machen sich fertig. Laura und Nadia are getting ready for a party at a friend's house. Complete their conversation with the correct forms of the following words.

anprobieren	leihen	stehen
drüben	passen (2x)	tragen (2x)
eng	schick	vergessen

NADIA: Du musst dich beeilen, Laura. Wir müssen in fünfzehn Minuten los!

LAURA: Ich weiß! Aber was soll ich (1) _____? Mein lila Rock hat einen großen Fleck (*stain*).

NADIA: Du kannst mein blaues Kleid tragen. Die Farbe Blau (2) _____ dir

sehr gut. Hier, (3) _____ es mal _____.

LAURA: Meinst du? Aber dein Kleid (4) _____ mir bestimmt nicht. Ich trage Größe 38. Das Kleid ist sehr schön, aber es ist mir sicherlich zu

(5) _____.

NADIA: Hmmm . . . Ich habe eine Idee. Den lila Rock kannst du noch

(6) _____, wenn du eine lange Bluse darüber (*over it*) trägst. Den Fleck sieht dann keiner.

LAURA: Das geht vielleicht. (7) _____ du mir deine schwarzen Stiefel? Meine Schuhe sind so alt und hässlich, deine Stiefel sind aber sehr

(8) _____.

NADIA: Natürlich. Sie stehen dort (9) _____ in der Ecke. Du darfst eine

warme Jacke auch nicht (10) _____. Das Wetter soll heute Abend kühl werden!

8-3 Kreuzworträtsel. Complete the crossword puzzle by finding the vocabulary words that correctly complete each sentence.

1. Man _____ eine Telefonnummer.

2. Christian fühlt sich allein. Er ist _____.

3. Geld hat man in einem _____.

4. Man bekommt eine _____ zu einer Hochzeit oder einer Party.

5. Ich kann nicht telefonieren, weil die Leitung _____ ist.

6. Ein Dialog oder ein Diskussion ist ein _____.

7. Man kauft Kleidung in einem _____.

8. Das Geschäft hat von 8.00 bis 18.00 Uhr _____.

9. Ich gehe in Urlaub. Kannst du meine Katze _____?

10. Bevor ich einkaufe, mache ich eine _____.

11. Man sucht im _____ nach einer Telefonnummer.

12. Am Telefon sagt man zum Abschied: _____!

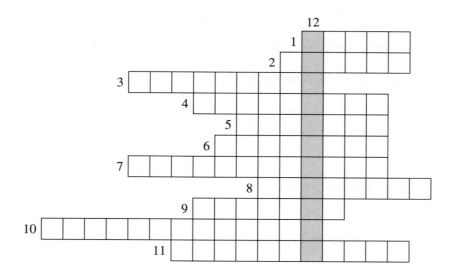

Schritte

8-4 Lotterie. Lothar just read an article in the newspaper about a family that won 10 million euros in the lottery. He discusses with his friends Ulrike and Julian what they would do with that much money.

☞ REVIEW SCHRITT 3: The **würde** construction

LOTHAR: 10 Millionen Euro! Das ist viel Geld! Was (1) _____ ihr mit so viel Geld tun?

ULRIKE: Ich (2) _____ nicht mehr studieren und nie wieder arbeiten!

Meine Freunde und ich (3) _____ um die Welt reisen und

exotische Länder besuchen. Was (4) _____ du damit machen,
Julian?

JULIAN: Ich (5) _____ meinen Eltern ein schönes, großes Haus auf dem

Land kaufen. Sie (6) _____ auch ein neues Auto und ganz neue
Möbel bekommen.

LOTHAR: Ihr (7) _____ nichts von dem Geld sparen? Ich

(8) _____ vielleicht nur eine Million ausgeben und den Rest

(*the rest*) investieren. So (9) _____ meine Familie auf immer
reich bleiben!

8-5 Was würden Sie tun? Use **würde** to indicate what you or others would do in the
following situations.

☞ REVIEW SCHRITT 3: The **würde** construction

BEISPIEL: Sie haben einen goldenen gefunden.
→ Ich würde ihn der Polizei geben.
ODER → Ich würde ihn verkaufen und mit dem Geld einen DVD-Spieler kaufen.

1. Sie bekommen in dem nächsten Deutschexamen ein D.

   _____

2. Ihre Eltern geben Ihnen kein Geld mehr.

   _____

3. Ihr(e) Mitbewohner(in) möchte nächste Woche ausziehen.

   _____

4. Ihre Lieblingshose hat plötzlich ein großes Loch.

   _____

5. Sie haben Ihr Portmonee verloren.

   _____

6. Ihr Telefon funktioniert nicht mehr.

   _____

8-6 Paulas Tagesablauf. Complete the sentences to find out what Paula does in the course of the day.

☞ REVIEW SCHRITT 6: Subordinating conjunctions

_____ 1. Paula geht ins Bad,

_____ 2. Sie duscht sich,

_____ 3. Obwohl sie nichts kaufen will,

_____ 4. Sie telefoniert mit ihrem Vater,

_____ 5. Sie erzählt ihrer Schwester,

_____ 6. Nachdem sie gegessen hat,

_____ 7. Sie fragt ihre Mitbewohnerin,

_____ 8. Am Abend bleibt sie zu Hause,

_____ 9. Wenn sie müde wird,

a. dass sie eine neue Arbeit gefunden hat.

b. bis es kein warmes Wasser mehr gibt.

c. spült sie das Geschirr.

d. bevor ihre Mitbewohnerin aufsteht.

e. geht sie ins Bett.

f. geht sie ins Kaufhaus.

g. ob sie ihr mit der Hausarbeit helfen kann.

h. damit sie ein Buch lesen kann.

i. weil er Geburtstag hat.

8-7 Über mich. Complete the following statements about yourself. Pay attention to word order.

☞ REVIEW SCHRITT 6: Subordinating conjunctions

1. **Als** ich 10 Jahre alt war, _____

_____

2. Ich lerne Deutsch, **weil** _____

_____

3. In diesem Deutschkurs habe ich gelernt, **dass** _____

_____

4. Ich möchte wissen, **ob** _____

_____

5. **Obwohl** ich Student(in) bin, _____

_____

6. **Nachdem** ich mein Studium absolviert (*completed*) habe, _____

_____

7. **Wenn** meine Freunde Geburtstag haben, _____

_____

8-8 Klatsch. You overhear a conversation between Udo and his girlfriend Trudi, and now you are telling a mutual friend what you heard. Since you missed the end of their conversation, you decide to embellish your story. How do you imagine their discussion ended?

☞ REVIEW SCHRITT 6: Subordinating conjunctions / Indirect statements and questions

UDO: Wohin gehen wir heute Abend?

TRUDI: Ich würde gern einen Film sehen.

UDO: Willst du ins Kino gehen?

TRUDI: Ich möchte lieber ein Video ausleihen.

UDO: Warum willst du nie ausgehen?

TRUDI: . . .

UDO: . . .

BEISPIEL: Udo fragt, wohin sie heute Abend gehen.

Trudi sagt, _____

Udo fragt, _____

Trudi sagt, _____

Udo möchte wissen, _____

_____

_____

_____

8-9 Udo und Trudis Verhältnis (*relationship*). Udo tells about his relationship with Trudi. Form complete sentences with the given elements. Pay attention to word order.

☞ REVIEW SCHRITT 8: Word order: time–manner–place

1. wir / kennen gelernt / auf einer Studentenparty / uns / letztes Jahr / an der Uni / haben

   _____

2. Trudi / mit mir / getanzt / hat / die ganze Nacht /

   _____

3. habe / am nächsten Tag / mit ihr / ich / telefoniert / stundenlang /

   _____

4. im Sommer / sind / zusammen / wir / in Urlaub / gefahren / für eine Woche

   _____

5. abends / wir / bleiben / zu Hause / oft

   _____

8-13 Ausreden (*excuses*). You find yourself having to make lots of excuses lately, both for things you have done and things you are trying to get out of doing. What excuses would you make in the following situations?

1. Ihre Eltern: "Ein F in Biologie! Wie ist denn das passiert?"
   Sie:

   _____

2. Ihr(e) Mitbewohner(in): "Warum hast du heute nicht aufgeräumt?"
   Sie:

   _____

3. Ein Bekannter: "Kommst du nicht zu meiner Party?"
   Sie:

   _____

4. Ihr(e) Professor(in): "Sie kommen heute sehr spät zur Deutschstunde!"
   Sie:

   _____

5. Ihr(e) Freund(in): "Als ich dich heute angerufen habe, warst du nicht zu Hause."
   Sie:

   _____

6. Zwei Freunde: "Wir hoffen, dass du uns am Samstag zum Flughafen fahren kannst."
   Sie:

   _____

Schaubild: Einkaufen online.

According to a recent study done by the *Institut für Demoskopie Allensbach,* Internet shopping is gaining popularity in Germany. Study the graphic containing data from the year 2002.

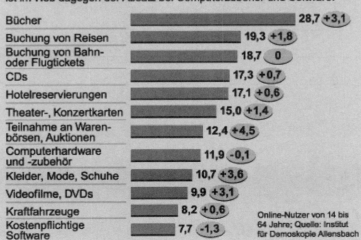

Aus "Medienspiegel", Nr. 11, Nov. 2002.

Quelle: Institut der deutschen Wirtschaft (Köln)

8-14 Wer kauft was im Web? Complete the summary analysis using information from the graphic.

2002 hat (1) _____ Prozent der Deutschen im Alter von

(2) _____ bis (3) _____ Jahren schon mal im

Internet eingekauft. Nummer eins auf der Liste der gekauften Produkte sind

(4) _____. Viele Deutsche haben auch ihren nächsten Urlaub mit

Hilfe des Internets geplant. (5) _____ Prozent der Käufer hat

übers Web ein Hotel reserviert. Und noch mehr Leute haben (6) _____,

(7) _____ oder (8) _____ gebucht. Unter den

Online-Käufern sind auch Musikfans zu finden. 17,3 Prozent der Surfer hat

(9) _____ gekauft und 15 Prozent hat (10) _____ fürs

Theater oder ein Konzert gekauft. Web-Surfer haben 2002 auch Hardware und Software

für den (11) _____ gesucht, aber weniger als im Jahre 2001.

8-15 Und selber? Answer the questions about your own attitudes toward and experiences with Internet shopping.

1. Wie oft kaufen Sie etwas übers Web?

   _____

2. Haben Sie schon mal etwas übers Internet gekauft? Wenn ja, was?

   _____

   _____

   _____

3. Was würden Sie im Internet nicht kaufen? Warum nicht?

   _____

   _____

   _____

Kultur

8-16 Kulturnotizen. Briefly answer the following questions in English based on the **Kulturnotizen** sections of **Kapitel 8**.

1. How might your current shopping habits change if you lived in a German-speaking country? Consider the differences from your own country in pricing, accepted forms of payment, store hours, and so on.

_____

_____

_____

_____

_____

_____

_____

_____

2. What are the advantages and disadvantages of having laws to regulate shopping hours as in the German-speaking countries?

_____

_____

_____

_____

_____

_____

_____

_____

3. Compare the German telephone system and phone etiquette with telephone usage in your own culture. Are there any notable differences?

_____

_____

_____

_____

_____

_____

_____

_____

8-17 Situationen. How would you respond in the following situations?

1. Sie sind im Modegeschäft und die Verkäuferin fragt: "Kann ich Ihnen helfen?" Sie sagen:

_____

2. Sie stehen an der Kasse im Kaufhaus und bezahlen einen Schal. Der Verkäufer fragt: "Sonst noch etwas?" Sie sagen:

_____

3. Sie sind zu Hause. Das Telefon klingelt. Sie nehmen den Telefonhörer ab und sagen:

_____

4. Sie wählen die Telefonnummer von einem Freund. Wenn sie nach Ihrem Freund fragen, sagt die Person am Apparat: "Ich glaube, Sie sind falsch verbunden." Sie sagen:

_____

5. Sie telefonieren mit einer Freundin. Bevor Sie den Telefonhörer auflegen, sagen Sie:

_____

9-7 Vergleiche. You're talking with a friend about your opinions on various topics. Compare each of the pairs of items or people. You may use each adjective only once.

☞ REVIEW SCHRITT 7: Comparative and superlative forms of adjectives and adverbs

BEISPIEL: Rindfleisch – Hähnchen
→ Hähnchen ist **gesunder als** Rindfleisch.
ODER Rindfleisch schmeckt mir **nicht so gut wie** Hähnchen.

1. ein BMW – ein Volkswagen

_____

2. Sommer – Winter

_____

3. ein Stuhl – ein Sessel

_____

4. Deutschland – die Schweiz

_____

5. Madonna – Britney Spears

_____

6. Sie – Ihre Eltern

_____

7. Ihr Zimmer – ?

_____

8. Deutsch – ?

_____

9-8 Superlative. A new exchange student is asking for your advice about your town and university. Tell her where she can find, for example, the cheapest clothes, the nearest supermarket, and help her avoid the most expensive food, the most uninteresting professors, and so on. Remember to use adjective endings. Use each adjective only once.

gut	schlecht	interessant	langweilig	neu	schick
teuer	billig	schön	hässlich	intelligent	frisch
fett	gesund	lecker	nah	laut	?

BEISPIEL: Die lecker**sten** Nachspeisen findest du im "Café Maximilian".
Der schnell**ste** Imbiss ist "Der Wurstkönig" in der Treupfarrstraße.
Die unfreundlich**sten** Kellner arbeiten im Restaurant "Jack and Jill".

1. der Supermarkt

_____

2. die Hamburger

_____

3. das Frühstück

_____

4. der Kaffee

_____

5. die Kleidung

_____

6. die Bücher

_____

7. die Musik

_____

8. die ProfessorInnen

_____

9. ?

_____

10. ?

_____

9-9 Fragen über Fragen. You are on vacation in Germany and are chatting in an Internet-Café with your friends back home. They have lots of questions about the food! Respond using demonstrative pronouns.

☞ REVIEW SCHRITT 9: Demonstrative pronouns

BEISPIEL: Hast du **die Bratwurst** probiert?
Ja, **die** habe ich probiert.
ODER Nein, **die** habe ich nicht probiert. Ich esse kein Fleisch!

1. Hast du **den Kaffee** probiert?

_____

2. Hast du **deutsches Bier** getrunken?

_____

3. Hast du auch **türkische Gerichte** probiert?

_____

4. Ist **die deutsche Schokolade** süß?

_____

5. Kostet **der deutsche Wein** viel?

_____

6. Sind **die Preise** hoch?

_____

7. Schmeckt dir **der Käse**?

_____

Alles klar?

9-10 Essen wie ein König. Tomorrow is your birthday and you can eat whatever you want. What will you eat for breakfast, lunch, and dinner? Where? With whom? Use lots of adjectives to make the food sound appealing. Pay attention to adjective endings. Write eight to ten sentences.

BEISPIEL: Ich stehe spät auf und esse ein großes Frühstück zu Hause. Ich esse gebratenen Speck mit Eiern und trinke frisch gepressten Orangensaft und schwarzen Kaffee. Meine besten Freunde essen mit mir zusammen und sie spülen auch das schmutzige Geschirr, damit ich mich ausruhen kann. . . .

_____

_____

_____

_____

_____

_____

_____

_____

_____

_____

_____

9-11 Wo essen wir? You are in the **Altstadt** in Munich and see information about various restaurants in the brochure you received at the tourist bureau. Read the ads and answer the questions below.

- Restaurant Amadeo -
italienische Spezialitäten

Pizza, Pasta, Fleischgerichte
*ausgezeichnete italienische Küche mit wöchentlich
wechselnden Spezialitäten aus allen Regionen Italiens*

italienische Weine
*den klassischen Chianti, den trockenen Frascati, den
süßen Lambrusco und auch besondere Flaschen aus
unserem Keller*

Frauenstr. 15, zwischen Viktualienmarkt und
Isartor. Tel. (089) 421 532

<u>Öffnungszeiten:</u>
*Mo-Di/Do-Sa 11.30-15.00 Uhr   So 18.00- 1.00 Uhr
Mittwoch Ruhetag*

*Wir wollen, dass es Ihnen und
unserer Umwelt gut geht!*

Café Kleopatra
vegetarisches Vollwert Café
Marienstr. 4 / Tel. 089/32 21 09

- wechselndes, internationales Tagesgericht
- preiswerte Snacks und frische Salate
- Lebensmittel aus biologischem Anbau
- kalt gepresste Öle und Butter statt Fabrikfette
- frisch gemahlenes Vollkornmehl
- selbstgebackene Kuchen
- April bis Oktober, Eisbecher und Eisgetränke

Montag - Freitag
Frühstücksbuffet - 7.00 - 10.00 Uhr
Mittagsbuffet - 12.00 - 14.00 Uhr
Happy Hour - 16.30 - 18.30 Uhr

Samstag, Sonntag und an Feiertagen
Brunch - 9.00 - 13.00 Uhr

Essen zum Mitnehmen,
täglich Frühstück

Istanbul-Garten
der Dönerimbiss in der Fussgängerzone

Neuhauser Str. 27 - 80331 München
Telefon: 089/23 183 256
Telefax: 089/260 53 79
E-mail: doenergarten@muenchen.de

Selbstverständlich bieten wir **Döner!**
Aber wir haben auch türkische Pizzen, Hähnchen,
Salate u. heiße u. kalte Getränke

*schnell, lecker und zu günstigen Preisen
täglich von 10 bis 23 Uhr für Sie geöffnet*

*Das Istanbul-Garten-Team wünscht Ihnen
Guten Appetit!*

BIERGARTEN AM CHINESISCHEN TURM
der größte Biergarten der Stadt
Englischer Garten 7 - 80538 München
Tel. 089/72 35 35 - Fax 089/72 35 34

- original bayrische Schmankerl
- gemütliche, gepflegte Atmosphäre
- hausgemachte Suppen
- bayrische Wurstspezialitäten
- Biere aus 3 Brauereien, aber auch
  alkoholfreie Getränke

Prosit!

Öffnungszeiten
März - Okt: täglich von 19-1 h
Nov - Jan: Di-So 12-14, 16-23 h / Mo Ruhetag
Feb: Betriebsferien

1. Wo kann man vegetarisch essen?

   _____

2. Wo bekommt man italienische Spezialitäten?

   _____

3. Wo bekommt man Weißwurst?

   _____

4. Wo kann man frühstücken?

   _____

5. In welchem Restaurant kann man per E-Mail bestellen?

   _____

6. Wo bekommt man drei verschiedene Biersorten?

   _____

7. Es ist Mittwoch 11.30 Uhr morgens. Wo können Sie essen?

   _____

8. Es ist Sonntag 23.30 Uhr. Wo können Sie essen?

   _____

9. In welchem von diesen Restaurants würden Sie am liebsten essen? Warum?

   _____

   _____

   _____

   _____

   _____

9-12 Lesestück: Gesunder essen — gesunder leben. The text below offers some tips for
maintaining a well-balanced diet. Before you read for detail, skim the text and determine

which of the sub-headers below belongs with which section. Write the number of that section next to the header.

_____ Ballaststoffe, Ballaststoffe und wieder mal Ballaststoffe

_____ Gemüse und Obst — 5 am Tag

_____ Groß oder klein, Frühstück muss sein

_____ Ausreichend Wasser

_____ Tierische Proteine durch Fisch und Milchprodukte

_____ Vielseitig essen

_____ Wenig Fett und fettreiche Lebensmittel

_____ Zucker und Salz in Maßen

Gesunder essen — gesunder leben

Mit den acht einfachen Ernährungsregeln bieten Sie ihrem Organismus die besten Voraussetzungen für Gesundheit und Lebensqualität. Sie vermeiden Übergewicht[1] und Folgeerkrankungen wie Arteriosklerose oder Gicht[2]. Versuchen Sie, diese Tipps in ihrem Alltag umzusetzen. Es wird sich lohnen!

1. _____

Essen Sie Frühstück. Wer kein Frühstück essen kann oder mag, soll wenigstens ein Glas Fruchtsaft oder Milch trinken. Wer einfach keine Zeit hat, soll lieber eine halbe Stunde früher aufstehen, denn Frühstück ist das "Sprungbrett" in den Tag.

2. _____

Essen Sie viele ballaststoffreiche Kost wie Vollkorn-Produkte, Getreide, Getreideprodukte, Cornflakes, Müsli, Reis und Nudeln. Ihre tägliche Ernährung soll 30 Gramm enthalten. Sie geben Ihnen Energie und regulieren das Sättigungsgefühl[3]. Sie haben auch wichtige Nährstoffe[4] und enthalten kaum Fett.

3. _____

Essen Sie viel Gemüse und Obst, mindestens fünf Portionen am Tag, denn diese Lebensmittel sind kalorienarm und reich an Vitaminen, Mineralstoffen, Spurenelementen und Ballaststoffen. Gekocht oder roh, tiefgefroren oder frisch, wie Sie es am liebsten mögen oder es Ihnen am besten passt.

4. _____

Essen Sie fettarm, denn zu viel Fett macht dick und krank. Obwohl der Körper essentielle Fettsäuren[5] für das Leben braucht, essen die meisten Menschen viel zu viel Fett. Pro Tag braucht man maximal 60 Gramm. Essentielle Fettsäuren sind vor allem in Fisch und pflanzlichen Ölen wie z. B. Sonnenblumen- Soja-, Maiskeim- oder Olivenöl enthalten. Tierisches[6] Fett enthält Cholesterin, also essen Sie lieber Magervarianten[7] bei Fleisch, Wurst und Käse.

5. _____

Essen Sie nicht mehr als zwei- bis dreimal pro Woche Fleisch und wöchentlich nicht mehr als drei Eier. Einmal wöchentlich sollen Sie Fisch wie Forelle, Lachs oder Thunfisch essen, denn diese haben einen hohen Anteil an Omega-3-Fettsäuren. Auch pflanzliche Proteine, wie z.B. in Getreiden, Nüssen und Bohnen, und in Milchprodukten sind ein guter Baustoff für Ihre Organe und Muskeln.

6. _____

Reduzieren Sie die Menge an Süßigkeiten und Salz in Ihrer Ernährung. Zucker zerstört die Zähne und liefert keine Nährstoffe. Cola und andere gezuckerte Getränke sollen Sie nicht zu oft genießen. Zu viel Salz überdeckt den Eigengeschmack der Speisen und kann Bluthochdruck fördern.[8] Fünf Gramm täglich reichen aus. Nehmen Sie lieber frische Kräuter[9] und Gewürze und wenn Salz, dann Jodsalz.

7. _____

Trinken Sie pro Tag mindestens 1,5 Liter Wasser, Fruchtsäfte oder Früchte- bzw. Kräutertees. Wenn man krank ist, braucht man noch mehr. Kaffee, schwarzen Tee und alkoholische Getränke soll man nur in Maßen[10] trinken. Diese sind Genussmittel und keine Durstlöscher. Alkohol, in größeren Mengen konsumiert, kann sogar zur Droge werden und den Körper zerstören.

8. _____

Schließlich sollen Sie viele verschiedene Lebensmittel genießen. Es gibt keine gesunden, ungesunden oder verbotenen[11] Lebensmittel. Es kommt eher auf die Menge, Auswahl und Kombination der Lebensmittel an.

[1] excess weight [2] gout [3] feeling of satiation [4] nutrients [5] fatty acids
[6] from animals [7] lean or low-fat varieties [8] promote, cause [9] herbs
[10] in moderation [11] forbidden

9-13 Wie viel soll man essen? Based on the text, what amounts of the following foods are normal for a healthy diet?

_____ 1. Fett

_____ 2. Wasser

_____ 3. Salz

_____ 4. Ballaststoffe

_____ 5. Obst und Gemüse

_____ 6. Fleisch

_____ 7. Fisch

_____ 8. Eier

a. 5 Portionen täglich

b. 5 Gramm pro Tag

c. 30 Gramm pro Tag

d. 60 Gramm täglich

e. einmal pro Woche

f. zwei bis dreimal pro Woche

g. maximal drei Stück pro Woche

h. 1,5 Liter täglich

9-14 So is(s)t man gesund. Determine, based on the text above, if the following statements are true or false. Mark the true statements **R** (*richtig*) and the incorrect ones **F** (*falsch*).

_____ 1. Man muss jeden Tag ein großes Frühstück essen.

_____ 2. Getreideprodukte, Reis und Nudeln enthalten Ballaststoffe.

_____ 3. Gemüse soll man kochen, bevor man es isst.

_____ 4. Menschen brauchen Fett zum Leben.

_____ 5. Proteine kann man auch von Pflanzen bekommen.

_____ 6. Zu viel Zucker führt zu hohem Blutdruck.

_____ 7. Wenn man krank ist, soll man täglich mehr als 1,5 Liter Wasser trinken.

_____ 8. Fleisch und Fett sind verbotene Lebensmittel.

9-15 Essen Sie gesund? Look back at the food pyramid in **9-1** and reread the tips above, this time taking into account your own eating habits: Do you eat a balanced diet? Which tips do you already follow? Describe your eating habits, and explain what you should do to improve your nutrition. Write eight to ten sentences.

Nützliche Ausdrücke

Ich esse / trinke täglich . . .   Ich soll . . .
                                      Ich muss . . .

_____

_____

_____

_____

_____

_____

_____

_____

_____

_____

Kultur

9-16 Kulturnotizen. Briefly answer the following questions in English based on the **Kulturnotizen** sections of **Kapitel 9**.

1. How is grocery shopping in the German culture different from shopping for food in your culture? Or, if you have been grocery shopping in a German-speaking country, what similarities and differences did you notice compared with your own culture?

_____

_____

_____

_____

_____

_____

_____

_____

2. How are German meals different from or similar to those in your culture? How have eating traditions changed over the past decades—both in the German-speaking countries and in your own culture?

_____

_____

_____

_____

_____

_____

_____

_____

3. What unfamiliar customs might you encounter if you were to eat in a restaurant in a German-speaking country? Or, if you have experienced a restaurant meal in German culture, what was different from what you were used to?

_____

_____

_____

_____

_____

_____

_____

9-17 Situationen. How would you respond in the following situations?

1. Sie wollen ins Kino gehen, aber Sie haben großen Hunger. Der Film beginnt in

   15 Minuten. Wo können Sie schnell etwas essen? _____

2. Sie gehen in ein Restaurant. Alle Tische sind besetzt. Eine Dame sitzt aber allein an

   einem Tisch für vier Personen. Sie gehen hin und fragen: _____

3. Sie sitzen am Tisch und sehen sich die Speisekarte an. Nach ein paar Minuten
   entscheiden Sie sich, was Sie essen möchten, und wollen den Kellner herbeirufen

   (*summon*). Sie sagen: _____

4. Sie gehen mit Freunden essen. Nachdem Sie bestellt haben, bringt die Kellnerin das

   Bier. Bevor Sie trinken, sagen Sie: _____

5. Wenn das Essen kommt, sagt Ihre Freundin: "Guten Appetit!" Sie

   sagen: _____

6. Sie sind im Restaurant. Sie haben schon gegessen und möchten jetzt die Rechnung

   haben. Sie sagen dem Kellner: _____

7. Ihr Essen kostet €14,30. Sie geben dem Keller €15,-- und

   sagen: _____

Drei Kellner-Witze

GAST: "Aber Herr Ober, der Kaffee ist ja kalt!"
OBER: "Gut, dass Sie mir das sagen, mein Herr! Eiskaffee kostet nämlich einen Euro mehr . . ."

GAST: "Was würden Sie mir empfehlen?"
OBER: "Das Restaurant zwei Häuser weiter."

GAST: "Herr Ober, in meiner Suppe schwimmt eine tote Fliege!"
OBER: "Unsinn, tote Fliegen können gar nicht schwimmen!"

Erweiterung

More on adjective endings: Indefinite numerical adjectives

Indefinite numerical adjectives do just what their name suggests: they indicate indefinite amounts. You have already learned many of them as individual vocabulary words; these are words that mean *many, some, a few,* and so on. They fall into two categories: singular and plural.

Singular indefinite adjectives

genug	*enough*	**wenig**	*little; a small amount of*
etwas	*some*	**viel**	*much; a lot of*
mehr	*more*		

The singular indefinite adjectives are typically used with singular nouns. They are undeclined, that is, they do not take adjective endings. Any other adjectives are declined regularly:

Meine Eltern haben **wenig** Geld.	*My parents have little money.*
Würdest du mir bitte **etwas** Brot geben?	*Would you please give me some bread?*
Ich esse **viel** frisch**es** Obst.	*I eat a lot of fresh fruit.*

Plural indefinite adjectives

ander-	*other*	**wenige-**	*(a) few*
einig-	*some, several*	**viel-**	*many*
mehrer-	*several*		

The plural indefinite adjectives are generally used with plural nouns. They are declined like any other plural adjectives; when used without a **der-** or **ein-**word, they take the same endings as other unpreceded plural adjectives:

Einig**e** Vegetarier essen keine Eier.	*Some vegetarians don't eat eggs.*
In der Fußgängerzone habe ich viel**e** neu**e** Gaststätten gesehen.	*In the pedestrian zone I saw many new restaurants.*
Keine ander**en** Gerichte sind so gut wie dieses Gericht.	*No other dishes are as good as this dish.*
Von **den** wenig**en** Vorspeisen habe ich keine gemocht.	*Of the few appetizers, I didn't like any.*

9-18 Auf dem Markt. Elise and Kai are at the market trying to decide what to buy. Complete their conversation using the cues with the correct indefinite adjectives. Supply the proper adjective endings where necessary.

ELISE: Was wollen wir kaufen?

KAI: Ich möchte (1) _____ (some) Fleisch. Wir haben nicht

(2) _____ (enough) Würstchen und ich will auch Aufschnitt fürs Frühstück.

ELISE: Lass uns erst mal (3) _____ (some) Obst kaufen, denn hier

sind wir gerade. Kaufen wir (4) _____ (some) Äpfel?

KAI: Wir haben zu Hause noch so (5) _____ (many) Äpfel, oder?

ELISE: Ja, aber die isst du nicht. Würdest du nicht lieber ein paar von den

(6) _____ (other) Äpfeln kaufen — Jonagold oder Elstar vielleicht?

KAI: Na, gut, Jonagold hört sich schön an.

ELISE: Wollen wir vielleicht auch (7) _____ (some) Nektarinen kaufen?

KAI: Ich weiß nicht. Ich weiß, ich soll (8) _____ (more) Obst

essen, aber hier sind so (9) _____ (few) Nektarinen und sie sehen etwas alt aus.

ELISE: Ja, die (10) _____ (other) Obstsorten (pl.) sehen frischer aus. Nehmen wir ein paar Pfirsiche.

KAI: O, nein. Lieber keine Pfirsiche. Die mag ich nicht.

ELISE: Du isst so (11) _____ (little) Obst, weil wir so selten Obst

kaufen. Wenn wir zu Hause (12) _____ (more) Obst haben, isst du vielleicht auch mehr.

KAI: Vielleicht hast du Recht.

ELISE: Wollen wir heute Abend einen Obstsalat machen? Hier gibt's noch

(13) _____ (several other) Obstsorten. Wir finden bestimmt etwas, was du magst.

KAI: OK. Kiwis, Erdbeeren und Bananen mag ich.

ELISE: Sehr gut. Und mit den Äpfeln dazu haben wir (14) _____ (enough) Obst für einen Obstsalat.

Unterwegs

Themenwortschatz

10-1 Europa. Find the German names of the 15 countries whose capitals are listed below.

Paris	Lissabon	Stockholm	Bern
Rom	Warschau	Athen	Moskau
Prag	Ankara	Wien	Brüssel
Dublin	Berlin	Sofia	

A	S	P	R	E	I	β	P	O	R	T	U	G	A	L	Ä	N	D	F	S
U	K	B	C	R	T	S	O	R	E	Ö	L	P	I	R	L	A	N	D	R
G	I	U	H	Q	B	E	L	G	I	E	N	G	R	I	E	P	D	E	U
R	R	L	U	Ü	G	G	E	C	H	T	U	O	Ö	F	S	Ü	R	I	D
I	F	G	E	H	C	U	N	G	Ä	R	W	P	R	S	C	C	G	L	E
E	T	A	F	R	A	N	K	R	E	I	C	H	T	G	H	T	S	F	U
C	G	R	B	Z	U	G	W	Ö	C	T	S	S	C	H	W	E	I	Z	T
H	W	I	T	R	S	K	R	T	V	A	X	N	M	H	E	O	S	Ä	S
E	S	E	Ü	S	T	M	F	I	J	L	B	I	S	J	D	F	D	Y	C
N	D	N	R	S	β	G	Ü	D	S	I	N	K	E	T	E	T	G	U	H
L	C	β	K	P	R	T	S	C	H	E	C	H	I	E	N	E	C	O	L
A	V	I	E	O	I	M	B	V	B	N	K	Ä	S	Y	Ü	R	B	Y	A
N	B	S	I	L	G	Ü	Ö	S	T	E	R	R	E	I	C	H	H	J	N
D	N	U	I	L	K	D	E	S	W	A	X	R	U	S	S	L	A	N	D

10-2 Claudia und Helmut planen einen Urlaub. Claudia and Helmut will be taking a vacation to California soon. Complete their conversation with the correct forms of the following words.

abfliegen	buchen	Meer	übernachten
abholen	Pension	Reisebüro	verbringen
ankommen	Koffer	reservieren	
Berge	Küste	Schlafsack	

CLAUDIA: Ich war heute im (1) _____ und habe unseren Flug nach

Kalifornien (2) _____.

HELMUT: Schön! Wann fliegen wir denn?

CLAUDIA: Morgen in drei Wochen. Wir (3) _____ um 12.30 vom

Frankfurter Flughafen _____ und

(4) _____ um 14.40 in San Francisco

_____. Nächste Woche muss ich die Tickets

(5) _____.

HELMUT: Hast du auch schon ein Hotelzimmer (6) _____?

CLAUDIA: Nein, noch nicht. Ich habe diese Broschüren mit nach Hause gebracht. Ich dachte, vielleicht könnten wir ein Zimmer in einer kleinen, romantischen

(7) _____ am (8) _____ finden.

HELMUT: Aber das würde bestimmt sehr viel Geld kosten, und wir werden nicht so viel

Zeit im Zimmer (9) _____, oder?

CLAUDIA: Vielleicht hast du Recht.

HELMUT: Ich dachte, wir wollten die (10) _____ entlang
fahren und auch in den Nationalparks in den schönen hohen

(11) _____ wandern.

CLAUDIA: Weißt du was? Wir sollten nicht im Hotel oder in einer Pension

(12) _____, sondern wir sollten eigentlich campen.

HELMUT: Ja, das ist eine tolle Idee! Nehmen wir lieber Rucksäcke als

(13) _____ und packen wir unser Zelt und unsere

(14) _____.

CLAUDIA: Klasse! Ich freue mich schon auf die Reise!

HELMUT: Ich mich auch!

10-10 Im Sommer. Which of these activities did you do during the summer when you were a child? Add extra information, where appropriate.

☞ REVIEW SCHRITT 7: The simple past tense

BEISPIEL: Geld verdienen
→   Ich verdiente als Babysitter Geld.
ODER   Ich verdiente kein Geld, weil ich zu jung war, einen Job zu haben.

1. mit Freunden spielen

_____

2. mit meiner Familie reisen

_____

3. im Meer schwimmen

_____

4. früh aufstehen

_____

5. Zeit mit meinen Großeltern verbringen

_____

6. Zitronenlimonade trinken

_____

7. krank werden

_____

8. Streit haben

_____

10-11 Im Wohnzimmer. Claudia is telling her friend Anika how she has rearranged her living room. Use **da**-compounds to complete the description.

☞ REVIEW SCHRITT 9: **da**- and **wo**-compounds

Helmut hat seinen Schreibtisch im Wohnzimmer. Darauf _____

_____

_____

_____

In dem Wohnzimmer haben wir unser Klavier. _____

_____

_____

_____

Wir haben einen neuen Wohnzimmertisch. _____

_____

_____

_____

10-12 Tante Rosa hört nicht richtig. You are telling Tante Rosa about Claudia and Helmut, but she doesn't hear everything. Using the bold-faced phrases, form questions using a **wo**-compound or a preposition + interrogative pronoun.

☞ REVIEW SCHRITT 9: **da-** and **wo**-compounds

BEISPIEL: Claudia und Helmut freuen sich **auf ihren Urlaub**.
→   **Worauf** freuen sie sich?

1. Claudia hat gestern **mit John** telefoniert.

   _____

2. Sie haben **über die Reise** geredet.

   _____

3. Er hat ihr **von der Stadt** erzählt.

   _____

4. Claudia hatte schon mal **von dem Kunstmuseum** gehört.

   _____

5. Sie regt sich **über die Reise** auf.

   _____

6. Claudia erinnert sich **an Johns Mutter**.

   _____

7. Johns Mutter erholt sich **von einer schweren Krankheit**.

   _____

8. Helmut fängt nach dem Urlaub **mit einer neuen Arbeit** an.

   _____

Ein Witz:

— "Wo warst du im Urlaub?"
— "In Berlin an der Nordsee."
— "Aber Berlin liegt doch gar nicht an der Nordsee."
— "Ach so. Deswegen mussten wir immer so weit zum Strand!"

Alles klar?

10-13 Eine Reise. Tell about a trip you took sometime in the past five years. Where did you go and why? What did you do and see there? With whom did you travel? Where did you stay? and so on. Write ten sentences using the simple past tense where appropriate.

_____

_____

_____

_____

_____

_____

_____

_____

_____

_____

_____

_____

_____

_____

10-14 Kieler Woche. You are planning to travel to Schleswig-Holstein for the *Kieler Woche*, an international sailing event that takes place every June in Kiel. You know rooms fill up fast, so you'd like to explore what accommodations are available before you go. Read the tourist information and answer the questions below.

Campingplatz-Fackelstein an der Ostsee

in der Nähe vom Olympiazentrum mit Blick auf die Kieler Förde, nur 10 Minuten von Kiel entfernt. Wasch- u. Sanitärräume, Strand in 100 m Entfernung, Einkaufen 4 km, Fahrradwege entlang dem Strand.

Preise pro Nacht:

Erwachsene - 4,35 €	Wohnmobil - 7,50 €
Kinder bis 14 J. - 2,85 €	Zelt nach Größe - 4,90 - 7,50 €
Hund / Katze - 1,90 €	Auto/Motorrad - 1,90 €
Tagesbesucher - 3,60 €	Solarium, 6 Min. - 3,10 €
Waschmaschine / Trockner - 2,60 €	

Geöffnet: April bis Oktober.
Tel/Fax: 0431 / 387 150. - cp-fackelstein@gmx.de

Ferienwohnung für 4 Personen

Erholung und Entspannung südlich der Landeshauptstadt Ruhige Lage nah am Wald, aber nur 20 km von der Kieler Innenstadt entfernt. 70 qm, 2 Schlafzimmer, Wohnzimmer, Küche, Dusche/WC, überdachte Terrasse, Garten, Gartenstühle, Grill. € 55 pro Tag.

Nach Vereinbarung stehen Ihnen zur Verfügung: Frühstücksservice (€ 5 pro Person), Bettwäsche und Handtücher, Kinderbett und Kinderhochstuhl, Waschmaschine und Wäschetrockner, Fahrräder (€ 5 pro Tag)

Anreisen erst ab 15.00 Uhr.
Tel. 0431 / 27 01 9
Familie Reinhard freut sich
auf Ihren Besuch!

Essen, Trinken, Schlafen und noch Meer! *Hotel am Strand*

Ob Urlaub oder Geschäftreise, Familienfeier oder Tagung können Sie sich freuen auf einen Aufenthalt in unserem Hotel am Strand mit traumhaftem Blick aufs Meer.

Alle Zimmer sind neu renoviert und sind ausgestattet mit Bad/Dusche, Radiowecker, Kabelfernsehen, Minibar und Telefon. Lift, Parkplätze und Garage vorhanden.

EZ Euro 85,-- bis 95,--
DZ Euro 105,-- bis 135,--
ganzjährig geöffnet

Strandstraße 42/44
24229 Strande
Tel. 04349/917 90
Fax. 04349/917 92 10

JUGENDHERBERGE KIEL

Johannesstraße 12
Tel./Fax. 0431 / 78 65 12
jhkiel@djh.de

~ vom Bahnhof 15 Min. zu Fuß
~ fantastischer Blick auf Kiel
~ 265 Betten in 2- u. 4-Bett Zimmern, teilweise rollstuhlfreundlich
~ neue Duschanlagen, jeweils 2 Zimmer teilen ein Waschbecken
~ geeignet für Schulklassen, Vereine, Familien, Einzelgäste

14,30 €, inkl. Frühstück
20.12. - 01.01. geschlossen
Hausvater: Robert Waldhauer

<table>
<tr><td>

Privatzimmer Kemper

Frau Kemper
Priwallstr. 34
24159 Kiel-Schilksee   Tel: 0431 / 15 98 02

Zimmer im Einfamilienhaus mit großem Garten in ruhiger
Lage. WC / Dusche im Flur. Bushaltestelle in der Nähe.
Wald und Sportplatz bieten Wander- und Jogging-
möglichkeiten. Generell Anreise erst ab 16.00 Uhr. Rufen
Sie vor der Ankunft bitte an! EZ 17,00 / DZ 27,00.

</td></tr>
</table>

1. Welche Unterkunft ist am teuersten? _____

2. Welche Unterkunft ist am billigsten? _____

3. Wo ist das Frühstück im Preis enthalten? _____

4. Wo gibt es Kabelfernsehen? _____

5. In welcher Unterkunft hat man eine Küche? _____

6. Wo dürfen Sie erst ab 16.00 Uhr ankommen? _____

7. Welche Unterkunft hat Zimmer mit vier Betten? _____

8. Welche Unterkunft ist in der Nähe von einem Wald? _____

9. Wo hat der Gast private Dusche und Toilette? _____

   _____

10. Sie sind gerade mit dem Zug in Kiel angekommen. Welche Unterkunft können Sie zu

    Fuß erreichen? _____

11. Welche Unterkunft kann man mit dem Bus erreichen? _____

12. Es ist Weihnachten und Sie suchen ein Zimmer für eine Nacht. Wo können Sie nicht

    übernachten? _____

    _____

10-15 Wo würden Sie übernachten? In different situations, people sometimes need different types of accommodations. Using the information in the ads in 10–14, where would you stay in each of the following situations?

1. Es ist Juni und Sie sind für die *Kieler Woche* in Kiel. Sie reisen allein und kennen niemanden in der Stadt. Wo möchten Sie übernachten? Warum?

   _____

   _____

   _____

   _____

2. Sie reisen mit 3 FreundInnen durch Europa und wollen eine Nacht in Kiel verbringen. Wo würden Sie übernachten? Warum?

   _____

   _____

   _____

   _____

3. Sie wollen in Schleswig-Holstein mit Ihrer Familie Urlaub machen. Sie wollen drei Wochen bleiben. Wo würden Sie übernachten? Warum?

   _____

   _____

   _____

   _____

Reisebericht: Unsere Fahrradtour durch Schleswig-Holstein

Andreas and his friend Hasan, both 17 years old and from the small village of Waldenau in Schleswig-Holstein, went on a six-day bike tour together last summer. As you read Andreas's travelogue, you can trace their route on the map. While reading, underline the names of the places that the teenagers passed through during their tour.

Letzten Sommer machte ich zusammen mit meinem Freund Hasan eine Fahrradtour durch Schleswig-Holstein. Dies war unser erster Urlaub ohne Eltern.

Donnerstag. Der erste Ort, den wir erreichten, war Siebeneichen, ein kleines Dorf am Elbe-Lübeck-Kanal. Als wir am Kanal entlang fuhren, sahen wir viele Schiffe. Der Weg führte uns weiter nach Mölln, einer sehr schönen Stadt mit vielen alten Häusern. Wir hielten an und kauften im Supermarkt etwas zu trinken und essen. Die erste Nacht verbrachten wir in Lübeck, wo wir sofort die Jugendherberge fanden.

Freitag. Wir gingen nach dem Frühstück und Getränkeeinkauf durch die Lübecker Innenstadt. Als wir aus der Stadt herausfuhren, mussten wir unseren ersten Berg hinauffahren. Von hier aus hatte man einen wunderschönen Blick auf die Stadt. Am Nachmittag konnten wir in Eutin einkaufen und da holte ich Geld von der Bank. Wir kamen dann endlich an die Ostsee und radelten die Küste entlang. In der Nähe vom Schönberger Strand fanden wir die Jugendherberge. Nachdem wir beim Italiener am Ort essen gingen, hatten wir vor, ins Bett zu gehen, aber in der Jugendherberge lernten wir vier Mädchen kennen und mit ihnen sprachen wir noch bis drei Uhr morgens.

Samstag. Wir fuhren auf dem Ostseeküstenradweg in Richtung Kiel weiter. Leider fing es an, sehr stark zu regnen, und wir zogen unsere Regenjacken an. Als wir etwa 2 Stunden später in Kiel ankamen, hörte der Regen auf. Am Nachmittag fuhren wir über den Nord-Ostsee-Kanal und in die Nähe des Kieler Flughafens. Da kamen wir an einer Landebahn vorbei, als gerade zwei Kampfflugzeuge aus den 50er Jahren landeten. Wir stiegen am Flughafen von unseren Fahrrädern ab und begaben uns ins Flughafen-Restaurant, wo Hasan einen Eisbecher bestellte und ich ein Stück Kuchen aß. Wir schliefen in Eckernförde, wo wir in der Jugendherberge zum ersten Mal ein kleines Zweibettzimmer für uns allein hatten.

Sonntag. Nach dem Frühstück fuhren wir gleich wieder los. Eine nette Frau erklärte uns den Weg bis zum nächsten Dorf. Es ging bergauf, bergab, bergauf, bergab und es wurde sehr windig. Wir kämpften mit starkem Gegenwind bis nach Husum, wo wir erst einmal ein Fischbrötchen aßen und Hasan 10 Euro im Wind verlor. Die Pension, wo wir übernachten wollten, lag noch 20 Kilometer entfernt. Obwohl wir keine Lust mehr hatten, radelten wir noch dahin. In der Pension freuten wir uns, unsere Schuhe ausziehen zu können. Ich fiel auf das sehr bequeme Doppelbett und schlief sofort ein.

Montag. Als wir aufwachten, schlug Hasan vor, dass wir einfach mit dem Zug direkt nach Hause fahren sollten. Er meinte, dass er sich bei diesem Wetter sofort einen Sonnenbrand holen würde. Trotzdem hielten wir uns an unseren Plan, mit dem Fahrrad weiter zu fahren. In dem nächsten Dorf kaufte sich Hasan ein langes Hemd gegen die Sonne. Dann kamen wir nach Friedrichsstadt und aßen in einem kleinen Gasthof zu Mittag. Noch drei Stunden Fahrt und wir hielten in Heide an, wo wir in einem Eiscafé Pause machten. In St. Michaelisdonn, unserem Ziel für den Tag, kamen wir früh an und konnten uns etwas ausruhen. Wir ließen unsere Rucksäcke in der Jugendherberge zurück und gingen spazieren.

Dienstag. Das Wetter war nicht ganz so gut wie während der letzten Tage. Es war bewölkt und kühl. Aber zum Fahrradfahren war das nicht unbedingt schlecht. Wir machten uns also auf den Weg in Richtung Zuhause und nahmen bei Kudensee die Fähre über den Nord-Ostseekanal. Auf der anderen Seite des Kanals kauften wir wieder ein und fuhren an der Elbe entlang. An diesem Tag trafen wir unterwegs sehr viele andere Radfahrer, die uns freundlich grüßten. Obwohl es 12 Uhr war, als wir in Glücksstadt ankamen, hatten wir noch keinen Hunger. Unser Ziel war ganz nah, deshalb radelten wir weiter. Gegen 17.00 Uhr kamen wir nach Waldenau, dem Ort, wo wir vor sechs Tagen unsere Tour begannen.

10-16 Wann ist das passiert? On which day of the week did each of the following things occur? Write the day of the week in the space provided.

Donnerstag   Freitag   Samstag   Sonntag   Montag   Dienstag

_____ 1. Es hat geregnet.

_____ 2. Andreas und Hasan haben vier Mädchen kennen gelernt.

_____ 3. Sie sind an die Ostsee gekommen.

_____ 4. Eine Frau hat ihnen den Weg erklärt.

_____ 5. Hasan hat sich ein Hemd gekauft.

_____ 6. Sie haben in einer Pension übernachtet.

_____ 7. Es ist sehr windig gewesen.

_____ 8. Andreas und Hasan haben viele andere Radfahrer getroffen.

_____ 9. Sie haben am Flughafen gegessen.

_____ 10. Hasan wollte den übrigen Weg mit dem Zug fahren.

_____ 11. Sie haben die Nacht in Lübeck verbracht.

_____ 12. Das Wetter war kühler als an den anderen Tagen.

_____ 13. Sie haben in einem italienischen Restaurant gegessen.

_____ 14. Sie sind an der Elbe entlang gefahren.

_____ 15. Abends sind Andreas und Hasan noch spazieren gegangen.

_____ 16. Sie haben Fischbrötchen gegessen.

_____ 17. Andreas hat Geld von der Bank geholt.

_____ 18. Hasan hat 10 Euro verloren.

10-17 Ruckblick. Answer the questions, providing information, where appropriate, from the text above to support your opinions.

1. Welcher Tag war Ihrer Meinung nach der beste Tag der Fahrradtour? Warum?

_____

_____

_____

_____

2. Welcher Tag war Ihrer Meinung nach der schlimmste Tag dieser Tour? Warum?

_____

_____

_____

_____

3. Erinnern Sie sich an Ihren ersten Urlaub ohne Ihre Eltern? Wohin sind Sie gefahren und was haben Sie da gemacht? Wie lange sind Sie weggeblieben?

_____

_____

_____

_____

Kultur

10-18 Kulturnotizen. Briefly answer the following questions in English based on the **Kulturnotizen** sections of **Kapitel 10**.

1. What are the most popular vacation choices of Germans? Why?

   _____

   _____

   _____

   _____

   _____

   _____

   _____

2. What are the advantages and disadvantages of staying in a youth hostel? Have you ever stayed in one or if not, would you consider staying there?

   _____

   _____

   _____

   _____

   _____

   _____

   _____

3. Why do you think train travel is more common in Europe than in North America?

_____

_____

_____

_____

_____

_____

_____

4. How is driving on a German **Autobahn** different from driving on highways and freeways in North America?

_____

_____

_____

_____

_____

_____

_____

10-19 Sehenswürdigkeiten. Label at least 12 of the geographical features listed on the map. See how many you can identify before consulting the map in *Alles klar?*.

WÄLDER: der Schwarzwald, der Thüringer Wald, der Teutoburger Wald

GEBIRGE: die Alpen, das Erzgebirge, das Harzgebirge, das Jura-Gebirge

BERGE: das Matterhorn, der Großglockner, die Zugspitze

FLÜSSE: der Rhein, die Mosel, die Donau, die Elbe

SEEN: der Bodensee, Genfer See, Chiemsee, Neusiedler See

MEERE: die Nordsee, die Ostsee

INSELN: die Ostfriesischen Inseln, Rügen, Helgoland, Sylt

1. _____   13. _____

2. _____   14. _____

3. _____   15. _____

4. _____   16. _____

5. _____   17. _____

6. _____   18. _____

7. _____ 19. _____

8. _____ 20. _____

9. _____ 21. _____

10. _____ 22. _____

11. _____ 23. _____

12. _____ 24. _____

Erweiterung

Countries, languages, and nationalities

In this **Kapitel**, you learned the German names of several countries. Throughout *Alles klar?*, you have also seen the names of some nationalities and languages. Many of the German names of countries, nationalities, and languages follow some basic patterns.

Countries

Countries are mostly neuter and singular:

(das) Deutschland	**(das) Russland**	**(das) China**
(das) Amerika	**(das) Spanien**	**(das) Ägypten**

Although they are neuter, they are usually not used with an article.

A few countries are feminine or plural, in which case the nouns are used with their article[1]:

die Schweiz	**die Tschechische Republik**	**die Niederlande** (*pl.*)
die Türkei	**die Slowakei**	**die USA** (*pl.*)

These articles must be declined when the country names take different cases: Wir kommen **aus der Slowakei**, Er wohnt **in der Schweiz**, and so on.

Languages

Most European language names, as well as many others, end in **-(i)sch**:

Deutsch	**Norwegisch**	**Arabisch**
Englisch	**Polnisch**	**Chinesisch**
Griechisch	**Ungarisch**	**Japanisch**

The language names are identical to the adjectives used to describe things or people from those countries, except that the equivalent adjectives are not capitalized in German (**deutsch, polnisch,** and so on).

---

[1]A very few countries—mostly located in the Middle East—are masculine and are normally used with the article: **der Iran, der Irak, der Libanon.**

Nationalities

The designation for a male citizen of a country often ends in the suffix **-er**. Occasionally an umlaut is added. The feminine counterpart retains the umlaut and adds an additional **-in.**

    der Amerikaner, - / die Amerikanerin, -nen
    der Kanadier, - / die Kanadierin, -nen
    der Engländer, - / die Engländerin, -nen
    der Japaner, - / die Japanerin, -nen
    der Mexikaner, - / die Mexikanerin, -nen
    der Spanier, - / die Spanierin, -nen

A handful of nationality designations for males end in **-e**. Occasionally an umlaut is added. The corresponding female term retains the umlaut but replaces the **-e** with **-in**. A few feminine forms add an umlaut although the masculine form does not have one.

    der Brite, -n / die Britin, -nen
    der Chinese, -n / die Chinesin, -nen
    der Däne, -n / die Dänin, -nen
    der Franzose, -n / die Französin, -nen
    der Schotte, -n / die Schottin, -nen
    der Schwede, -n / die Schwedin, -nen

A notable exception is the word for a German person:

    der Deutsche, -n   **die Deutsche, -n**

You will learn the reason for this difference in **Kapitel 11**.

10-20 Länder, Sprachen, Völker. Complete each sentence with the appropriate country name, nationality, or language. Be careful: not all countries have national languages that are derived from their country names!

1. Eine Griechin spricht _____.

2. Ein _____ kommt aus Frankreich.

3. Ein Türke spricht _____ und kommt aus

    _____.

4. In Dänemark spricht man _____.

5. Ein Italiener kommt aus _____ und spricht

    _____.

6. Eine _____ kommt aus Kanada und spricht

_____ oder _____.

7. Eine Britin kommt aus _____ und spricht

_____.

8. In Japan spricht man _____.

10-21 Persönliche Fragen. Answer the following questions in complete sentences.

1. Welche Länder haben Sie schon mal besucht? Was haben Sie da gemacht?

_____

_____

_____

_____

2. Welche Sprachen sprechen Sie?

_____

_____

3. Woher kommen Ihre Vorfahren (*ancestors*)?

_____

_____

4. Haben Sie ausländische Freunde? Wenn ja, woher kommen sie? Wo wohnen sie?

_____

_____

5. Was für ausländische Gerichte essen Sie gern?

_____

_____

11-10 Ein Märchen für Schüler. Complete the story below with the missing case endings. Where no ending is needed, leave the provided space blank.

☞ REVIEW SCHRITT 10: Nouns: Review and expansion / Review of case endings and functions

KAPITEL 9, SCHRITT 5: Adjective endings: Review and Expansion

Es war einmal (1) ein____ jung____ Schüler, der (2) ein____ bös____ Lehrerin hatte. Sie war sehr unfreundlich und trug immer nur (3) schwarz____ Kleidung. Alle (4) in ihr____ Klasse mussten (5) jed____ Tag viel arbeiten, weil sie (6) d____ Schülern so (7) viel____ Hausaufgaben gab. (8) D____ jung____ Schüler durfte nachmittags nicht (9) mit sein____ Freunden spielen, denn er durfte nicht (10) aus d____ Haus, bis (11) sein____ Hausaufgaben fertig waren. (12) Während d____ Stunde musste er (13) lang____ Aufsätze schreiben. Er sprach nicht (14) mit ander____ Schülern und achtete immer nur (15) auf d____ Lehrerin, weil er Angst vor ihr hatte.

(16) Ein____ Tages kam (17) d____ Lehrerin früh (18) in d____ Klassenzimmer und überraschte (19) d____ Kinder. (20) Anstatt ihr____ Buches nahm sie (21) aus ihr____ Tasche (22) ein____ groß____ Kuchen, den sie selbst gebacken hat. Sie sagte: "Weil ihr (23) dies____ Jahr so schwer gearbeitet und so viel gelernt habt, wollen wir heute (24) ein____ Party machen." (25) D____ Schüler waren alle froh und sie glaubten nicht mehr, dass (26) ihr____ Lehrerin böse war. (27) D____ jung____ Schüler dankte (28) sein____ Lehrerin, und meinte, dass er (29) im Laufe d____ Jahres doch viel gelernt hat.

11-11 Psychologen-Treff. Ulla and Heide are at a university get-together for psychology majors. Complete their conversation with the correct forms of the masculine weak nouns listed below.

☞ REVIEW SCHRITT 10: Nouns: Review and expansion / Weak nouns

Absolvent	Herr	Psychologe
Autor	Name	Student

ULLA: Heide, siehst du den Mann dort?

HEIDE: Meinst du den (1) _____ mit dem grauen Anzug?

ULLA: Ja, er ist ein sehr bekannter (2) _____. Er hat viele Bücher geschrieben.

HEIDE: Du liebe Zeit! Wie heißt er denn?

ULLA: Er heißt Manfred Koch. Er ist (3) _____ dieser Universität.

HEIDE: Woher kennst du ihn, Ulla? Die meisten (4) _____ kennen

seinen (5) _____ wohl nicht.

ULLA: Ich habe alle seine Bücher für meine Diplomarbeit gelesen. Er schreibt nämlich über die Psychologie der Kinder.

HEIDE: Weißt du, was er hier an unserer Universität macht?

ULLA: Ich habe irgendwo gelesen, dass er morgen im großen Hörsaal eine Rede hält. Er

spricht über den Beruf des (6) _____ im 21. Jahrhundert.

11-12 Minidialoge. Complete each of the brief dialogues below with an adjectival noun formed from an adjective in the list below. Make sure to use the appropriate endings.

☞ REVIEW SCHRITT 10: Nouns: Review and expansion / Adjectives used as nouns

| bekannt | deutsch | verwandt |
| best | klein | süß |

1. **ELKE:** Kennst du Paul?

   GERT: Ja, er ist ein _____ von mir.

2. **GERT:** Hast du gehört? Elke hat letzte Woche ein Kind bekommen. Sie hat jetzt einen Sohn.

   PAUL: Tatsächlich? Wie geht es dem _____?

3. **GERT:** Wer kommt am Samstag zu der großen Party?

   ELKE: Viele Freunde und auch einige _____: meine Eltern und meine beiden Schwestern.

4. **PAUL:** Ich habe dir etwas _____ gebracht — Kekse und Schokolade.

   ELKE: Ach, wie toll! Wie hast du gewusst, dass ich Süßigkeiten so gerne mag!

5. **ELKE:** Du arbeitest nun als Lehrer, oder?

   PAUL: Ja, und das _____ an dem Beruf ist, dass ich den Sommer frei habe.

6. **GERT:** Ist Pauls Frau Österreicherin?

   ELKE: Nein. Sie kommt aus München. Sie ist _____.

Alles klar?

11-13 Übersetzen Sie. You are excited about the history course you are taking this semester. Translate the following sentences into German.

1. This semester I'm taking a very interesting course.

   _____

2. I can't remember the name of the professor.

   _____

3. He has written a book about the history of the 18th century.

   _____

4. Next week, I have to give a report about Goethe and Schiller.

   _____

5. At the end of the semester there is a final exam.

   _____

6. He will probably notice that I have read his book.

   _____

11-14 Ihr Studium: Persönliche Fragen. Answer in complete sentences the following questions about your life as a student.

1. Was studieren Sie? Warum?

   _____

   _____

2. Welche Kurse belegen Sie dieses Semester? Was müssen Sie für Ihre Kurse machen (Referate, Aufsätze, Seminararbeiten, Prüfungen, Hausaufgaben, usw.)?

   _____

   _____

   _____

   _____

   _____

3. Wie bereiten Sie sich auf eine große Klausur vor?

   _____

   _____

4. Was machen Sie während der Semesterferien?

_____

_____

11-15 Nach dem Studium. What do you think your life will be like in five years? Describe your job, and speculate where you will likely live and work, whether you will have a family, what you will own, how you will live, and so on. Write eight to ten sentences.

BEISPIEL: In fünf Jahren werde ich wohl in New York City wohnen. Ich werde verheiratet sein, aber keine Kinder haben . . . .

_____

_____

_____

_____

_____

_____

_____

_____

_____

_____

_____

_____

_____

_____

Lesestück: Bildungswege für Gymnasiasten.

The career options for *Abiturienten* are broader than ever before. Read about the future plans of five students in the 13th grade at the *Geschwister-Scholl-Gymnasium*. As you read, underline words and phrases that indicate the educational and career path each pupil intends to follow.

"Ich interessiere mich schon immer für Technik und Naturwissenschaften und wollte schon seit meiner Kindheit Tierärztin werden. Da ich nun aber älter und eben auch realistischer bin, weiß ich, dass ich einen Beruf wählen muss, der mir gute Berufsaussichten bietet. Mir scheint der Maschinenbau ein Fach zu sein, das viele Möglichkeiten hat. Ich studiere an einer Fachhochschule, denn ein Universitätsstudium dauert mir viel zu lange — in der Regel 12 Semester! Außerdem scheint mir das zu theoretisch. An einer FH dauert es bis zum Abschluss nur halb so lang und dazu bekomme ich während des Studiums auch praktische Erfahrung. Und mit dem Diplom kann ich auch eher Karriere machen als mit einer Berufsausbildung."

Konstanze E.

"Ich bin bis zur 10. Klasse an der Realschule gewesen, dann habe ich aufs Gymnasium gewechselt, um das Abitur nachzuholen[1]. Die Ausbildungsberufe im Bereich der Informationstechnologie interessieren mich sehr. Im Moment habe ich vor, eine Ausbildung als Telekommunikationstechniker zu machen. Ich glaube, dieser Beruf hat Zukunft. Viele Leute fragen mich, warum ich das Abitur gemacht habe, wenn ich nicht studieren will. Das ist eben, weil ich mir alle Möglichkeiten offen[2] halten will. Vielleicht werde ich später doch noch studieren, und mit dem Abitur steht mir das noch offen."

Holger T.

"Meine Mutter ist Krankenpflegerin, mein Vater hat sich vor einigen Jahren zum Altenpfleger umschulen lassen[3]. Somit habe ich schon seit der Kindheit Interesse an den Gesundheitsberufen. Weil ich Kinderarzt werden möchte, ist 'Ausbildung oder Uni?' keine Frage für mich. Ich werde im Wintersemester mit einem Medizinstudium in Marburg beginnen. Als Studierender werde ich Freiheiten haben, die man als Azubi gar nicht hat. Und wenn ich mein Berufsziel endlich erreiche, werde ich einen hohen sozialen Status genießen.[4]"

Stefan F.

"Ich bin oft mit meinen Eltern auf Reisen gewesen und die Atmosphäre in Hotels hat mich immer fasziniert. Seitdem ich letztes Jahr ein Schülerpraktikum in einem Hotel gemacht habe, weiß ich, dass ich eine Ausbildung als Hotelfachfrau absolvieren will. Ich will keinen Bürojob, sondern etwas Praktisches machen. Nach der Ausbildung kann ich direkt in den Beruf einsteigen. Man meint, dass Abiturienten alle studieren müssen, aber ich stelle mir vor, dass eine Hotelfachfrau mit Abi-Abschluss auch besondere Vorteile hat. Außerdem: Wenn man eine abgeschlossene Berufsausbildung hat, stehen einemviele Weiterbildungsmöglichkeiten offen. Das gefällt mir."

Carolin W.

"Ich reise gern und interessiere mich für Sprachen, aber was ich nach der Schule machen will, weiß ich noch nicht. Ehrlich gesagt, habe ich große Angst vor der Zukunft. Was passiert, wenn ich mich für einen Beruf entscheide, der mir nach fünf Jahren keinen Spaß mehr macht? Das ist meinem Vater passiert, und seine Umschulung zum Fachinformatiker hat viel Zeit und Geld gekostet. Ich glaube, ich werde erst einmal ein Jahr in Australien oder Neuseeland verbringen, um mein Englisch zu verbessern und um dort Erfahrungen zu sammeln. Und danach? Wer weiß?"

Birgit R.

---

[1]*nachholen* = to make up [2]*open* [3]*umschulen lassen* = to get retrained [4]*enjoy*

11-16 Wer macht was? Complete each sentence with the correct name based on the students' statements on the previous page.

    Holger   Konstanze   Birgit   Carolin   Stefan

1. _____ wird in Marburg studieren.

2. _____ hat einen Realschulabschluss.

3. _____ hat Angst vor der Zukunft.

4. _____ interessiert sich für die IT-Berufe.

5. _____ will eine Ausbildung zur Hotelfachfrau absolvieren.

6. _____ möchte Arzt werden.

7. _____ wollte früher Ärztin werden.

8. _____ möchte besser Englisch sprechen.

9. _____ hat noch während der Schulzeit ein Praktikum gemacht.

10. _____ freut sich auf einen hohen sozialen Status im Beruf.

11. _____ will gar nicht an einer Hochschule studieren.

12. _____ will Maschinenbau studieren.

13. _____ wird nach dem Studium das Diplom bekommen.

14. _____ wird nach der Ausbildung vielleicht noch studieren.

11-17 Fragen zu den Bildungswegen. Answer the questions based on the information provided in the students' statements. Answer in your own words and use complete sentences.

1. Warum findet Constanze ein Studium an einer Fachhochschule besser als ein Universitätsstudium?

   _____

   _____

2. Was will Holger werden? Warum?

   _____

   _____

3. Warum interessiert sich Stefan für einen Beruf im Gesundheitsbereich?

   _____

   _____

4. Warum hat sich Carolin entschieden, Hotelfachfrau zu werden?

   _____

   _____

5. Wofür interessiert sich Birgit? Was meinen Sie: welche Berufe würden ihr gut gefallen?

_____

_____

6. Warum haben Sie sich nach der Schule für ein Studium entschieden? Welche anderen Möglichkeiten hatten Sie?

_____

_____

_____

_____

Kultur

11-18 Kulturnotizen. Briefly answer the following questions in English based on the **Kulturnotizen** sections of **Kapitel 11**.

1. How is primary and secondary education in German-speaking countries different from that in your own country? Describe at least three concrete differences.

_____

_____

_____

_____

_____

_____

_____

2. How does higher education in German-speaking countries differ from that of your own country? Describe at least three concrete differences.

_____

_____

_____

_____

_____

_____

_____

_____

3. If you lived in a German-speaking country, what educational and career path would you follow? What kind of training would you need and which schools would you likely need to attend?

_____

_____

_____

_____

_____

_____

_____

_____

11-19 Bildungswege: Wie sagt man das? Because of the unique structure of the German system of education, many specialized terms exist. Find the appropriate term for each definition, and include the articles.

Abitur	Fachhochschulreife	Pädagogische Hochschule
Azubi	Grundstudium	Schein
Diplom	Hochschulen	Staatsexamen
Doktorgrad	Magister	Studiengebühren
	Magisterarbeit	Zensuren

1. in dem Schulzeugnis _____

2. der Abschluss einer Realschülerin _____

3. der Abschluss eines Gymnasiasten _____

4. ein Lehrling in einem Ausbildungsberuf _____

5. vor dem Hauptstudium _____

6. TUs, PHs, FHs, Unis, usw. _____

7. Hochschule für LehrerInnen _____

8. die Kosten eines Studiums _____

9. Nachweis der Teilnahme an einem Kurs _____

10. der Abschluss eines Philosophen _____

11. der Abschluss einer Ingenieurin _____

12. Examen für LehrerInnen und JuristInnen _____

13. die Diplomarbeit eines Magisterkandidaten _____

14. der Abschluss einer Doktorandin _____

Erweiterung

More on nouns

In **Kapitel 9**, you learned that nouns can be created from the infinitive forms of verbs. Such verbs are always neuter in gender and their meanings are usually equivalent to the *-ing* form in English:

das Schlafen	*sleeping*	das Warten	*waiting*
das Einkaufen	*shopping*	das Segeln	*sailing*

In addition, many nouns in German are formed from verb stems. You have already learned several of these:

antworten	*to answer*	→	die Antwort	*answer*
arbeiten	*to work*	→	die Arbeit	*work*
besuchen	*to visit*	→	der Besuch	*visit*
erfahren	*to experience*	→	die Erfahrung	*experience*
vorschlagen	*to suggest*	→	der Vorschlag	*suggestion*
einladen	*to invite*	→	die Einladung	*invitation*
erzählen	*to tell, narrate*	→	die Erzählung	*narrative*

As you can see from these examples, some nouns are formed directly from the infinitive verb stem (infinitive minus **-en**), while others add **-ung** to the stem. In addition, sometimes the simple past or perfect tense stems become the basis for a noun. You know some of these as well:

anbieten	*to offer*	→	das Angebot	*offer*
sprechen	*to speak*	→	die Sprache	*language*
schenken	*to give as a gift*	→	das Geschenk	*present, gift*
spazieren gehen	*to go for a walk*	→	der Spaziergang	*walk, stroll*

Being aware of these relationships can help you sometimes to predict the meanings of nouns you have never seen before.

11-20 Neue Vokabeln. Create new nouns by adding **-ung** to the infinitive stem of each of the following verbs. Include the definite article. Then guess the meaning of the new word.

BEISPIEL: verschieben
→ die Verschiebung – postponement

1. reservieren _____

2. überraschen _____

3. vorbereiten _____

4. erinnern _____

5. entscheiden _____

6. beschreiben _____

7. bemerken _____

8. öffnen _____

11-21 Was bedeutet das? Below are some nouns that are formed from the stems of verbs that you have learned. Can you predict their meanings? Look them up only after you have attempted to guess their meanings.

BEISPIEL: der Unterricht
→ teaching, instruction

1. der Schlaf _____

2. der Tanz _____

3. der Beginn _____

4. die Schminke _____

5. der Schrei _____

6. der Biss _____

7. der Unterschied _____

8. der Sprung _____

9. der Sitz _____

10. die Auswahl _____

Alles klar?

12-15 Ihre Mediennutzung. Answer each of the following questions in two to three sentences.

1. Welche Kommunikationsmittel benutzen Sie am häufigsten?

   _____

   _____

2. Wie unterhalten Sie sich in Ihrer Freizeit?

   _____

   _____

3. Welche Fernsehsendungen haben Sie als Kind gern gesehen?

   _____

   _____

4. Was für Sendungen sehen Sie heute im Fernsehen?

   _____

   _____

5. Wie heißt Ihr Lieblingsfilm?

   _____

   _____

6. Was ist Ihr Lieblingsbuch? Wer ist der Schriftsteller / die Schriftstellenn?

   _____

   _____

7. Woher bekommen Sie Ihre Nachrichten?

   _____

   _____

8. Wann und wo hören Sie Musik? Was für Musik hören Sie gern?

   _____

   _____

12-16 Übersetzen Sie. Robert's mother worries constantly about him. Give the English equivalents of the following sentences.

1. Wenn er nur gesunder essen würde!

   _____

2. Das Hauptfach, das er gewählt hat, interessiert ihn nicht mehr.

   _____

3. An seiner Stelle hätte ich dieses Semester keine Seminare belegt.

_____

4. Wenn er ein Händy hätte, könnte er uns öfter anrufen.

_____

5. Ich hätte Lust, ihn zu besuchen.

_____

6. Er bereitet sich auf die Prüfung vor, die er nächsten Monat ablegen muss.

_____

Lesestück: Was deutschen Kindern wichtig ist

A recent survey of German youth revealed the relative importance of various media in their daily lives. As you read, underline the forms of media that are mentioned in the text.

Was deutschen Kindern wichtig ist

"Was würdest du auf eine einsame Insel mitnehmen?" Diese Frage beantworteten Kinder zwischen 6 und 13 Jahren in einer Umfrage des TV-Senders FoxKids. Überraschend ist, dass nur 1 Prozent der Kinder überhaupt an Essen und Trinken dachte. Ungeschlagen auf Platz eins landete mit 32 Prozent der Fernseher. Ohne ihr TV-Programm können sich deutsche Kinder eine einsame Insel nicht vorstellen. Weit dahinter rangierten Bücher (12 Prozent) und Computer (12 Prozent). Playstation, Gameboy und Radio wollten jeweils 8 Prozent mitnehmen, transportable CD-Spieler oder Walkman 7 Prozent. Die Gesellschaft[1] der Eltern wünschten sich nur 3 Prozent, zumindest[2] auf einer einsamen Insel.

In den letzten Jahrzehnten ist der Glotzkasten also zum "Familienmitglied" geworden. 99 Prozent aller deutschen Haushalte haben Fernsehen und viele Kinder besitzen sogar ein eigenes Fernsehgerät. Ein Haushalt empfängt durchschnittlich 33 TV-Sender und fast alle Programme bieten Sendungen rund um die Uhr. Als Lieblingssendungen nennen Jugendliche meist Serien und Spielfilme. Bei Mädchen kommen häufiger Seifenopern und bei Jungen dagegen Actionfilme vor. 87 Prozent sehen "häufig" oder "öfters" TV, 70 Prozent sogar täglich. Insgesamt verbringen Kinder im Durchschnitt rund 100 Minuten pro Tag vor der Glotze. Die sogenannten Vielseher, die das durchschnittliche tägliche Fernsehkonsum nach oben treiben, sitzen drei Stunden und mehr vor der Flimmerkiste. Einige Forscher[3] sind sogar der Meinung, dass viele Schulabgänger bis Ende der Schulzeit mehr Stunden vor dem Fernseher als in der Schule verbracht haben. Mehrere Studien zeigen also, dass Fernsehen an der Spitze aller Freizeitaktivitäten von Jugendlichen steht. Die Erwachsenen übertreffen[4] die Kinder allerdings: Nach dieser Studie liegt ihr täglicher TV-Konsum mit zirka 200 Minuten doppelt so hoch wie der der Kinder.

Auch wenn die Medienangebote vielfältiger geworden sind, dem Fernsehen hat es nicht geschadet. Mit dem Computer und Spielen wie dem Gameboy oder der Playstation verbringen deutsche Kinder nur etwa 50 Minuten pro Tag. Die tägliche Fernsehdauer hat sich in den letzten Jahren kaum verändert, sie ist sogar leicht gestiegen. Im internationalen Vergleich rangieren deutsche Kinder dabei auf Platz 12 von mehr als 50 untersuchten Ländern. Spitzenreiter sind Jugendliche in Mexiko (175 Minuten täglich), vor denen in den USA (170 Minuten täglich) und Polen (160 Minuten täglich).

[1]company   [3]researchers
[2]at least   [4]exceed, outdo

12-17 Richtig oder falsch? Determine, based on the text above, if the following statements are true or false. Mark the true statements **R** (*richtig*) and the incorrect ones **F** (*falsch*). Edit each of the untrue statements to make them true.

_____ 1. Fernsehen ist den Kindern wichtiger als Computer und Bücher.

_____ 2. Deutsche Kinder brächten lieber Bücher auf die Insel mit als einen Discman oder Walkman.

_____ 3. Wenn sie auf einer einsamen Insel leben müssten, nähmen Kinder am liebsten ihre Eltern mit.

_____ 4. 33 Prozent aller deutschen Haushalte hat einen Fernseher.

_____ 5. Jugendliche sehen am liebsten Zeichentrickfilme.

_____ 6. 70 Prozent der Kinder sehen jeden Tag fern.

_____ 7. Wöchentlich sehen deutsche Kinder etwa 100 Minuten fern.

_____ 8. Im Durchschnitt sehen Eltern öfter fern als ihre Kinder.

_____ 9. Wegen solcher Spiele wie Gameboy und Playstation ist das Interesse am Fernsehen in den letzten Jahren leicht gefallen.

_____ 10. Amerikanische Kinder sehen öfter als deutsche Kinder fern.

12-18 Das Fernsehen. In German-speaking countries, as in many industrialized societies, television is a dominant part of many people's lives. Answer the questions below.

1. Wie sagt man "television set" auf Deutsch? Finden Sie im Text oben sechs Synonyme dafür und listen Sie sie hier auf.

_____   _____

_____   _____

_____   _____

2. Im Text steht der Satz: Der Fernseher ist zum "Familienmitglied" geworden. Erklären Sie, was das bedeutet.

_____

_____

_____

_____

_____

3. Hat das Fernsehen eher einen positiven oder einen negativen Einfluss (*influence*) auf das Leben? Erklären Sie Ihre Antwort.

_____

_____

_____

_____

_____

12-19 Was würdest du mitnehmen? What three items would you choose to take with you to a deserted tropical island for a year-long stay? Discuss why you would choose these three things. Write ten sentences. You may choose to begin as follows: **Wenn ich ein Jahr auf einer einsamen Insel verbringen sollte, würde ich . . .**

_____

_____

_____

_____

_____

_____

_____

_____

_____

_____

_____

_____

_____

Kultur

12-20 Kulturnotizen. Briefly answer the following questions in English based on the **Kulturnotizen** sections of **Kapitel 12**.

1. How has German television changed over the past few decades?

_____

_____

_____

_____

_____

_____

_____

2. What specific similarities and differences exist between German and North American television programming?

_____

_____

_____

_____

_____

_____

_____

_____

3. Examine the graphic below. In what ways does it confirm what you have learned about the Germans? Why might these particular topics be of interest to them? In addition, what does the graphic reveal about their preferred Internet uses? (If you need help determining what the search items are, you could go to www.google.de and conduct the same searches yourself!)

Quelle: Google, aus Focus, 02/03 vom 06.01.2003

_____

_____

_____

_____

_____

_____

_____

_____

_____

_____

12-21 Deutsche Kunst und Kultur. Germans have made countless international contributions to the arts over the centuries, especially in the areas of music, literature, and film. Of the artists and works listed in the chart on the next page, how many do you already know? Write each number from the chart next to the item that belongs there.

_____ *All Quiet on the Western Front*

_____ Bertolt Brecht

_____ "Der Himmel über Berlin"

_____ "Der König der Löwen"

_____ "Der Tod in Venedig"

_____ "Der Triumph des Willens"

_____ die Brüder Grimm

_____ "Die Dreigroschenoper"

_____ Erich Maria Remarque

_____ Filmkomponist

_____ Film

_____ Filmmusik

_____ Gedicht

_____ Günter Grass

_____ Hans Zimmer

_____ Heinrich Heine

_____ "Kinder- und Hausmärchen"

_____ Komponist

_____ Leni Riefenstahl

_____ Ludwig van Beethoven

_____ Märchensammlung

_____ Propagandafilm

_____ Regisseur

_____ Roman

_____ *Run, Lola, Run*

_____ Schauspielerin

_____ Schriftsteller

_____ Stummfilm

_____ *Symphony No. 9*

_____ *The Magic Flute*

_____ *The Tin Drum*

_____ Thomas Mann

_____ Wolfgang Amadeus Mozart

Jahr	Name	Beruf	deutscher Titel	englischer Titel	Genre
1791	1	Komponist	"Die Zauberflöte"	2	Oper
1812/15	3	Sprachforscher	4	Children's and Household Tales	5
1822–24	6	7	"Sinfonie Nr. 9"	8	Sinfonie
1823	9	Schriftsteller	"Die Lorelei"	Lorelei	10
1912	11	Schriftsteller	12	Death in Venice	Novelle
1927	Fritz Lang	13	"Metropolis"	Metropolis	14
1928	15	16	17	Three-Penny Opera	Theaterstück
1929	18	Schriftsteller	"Im Westen nichts Neues"	19	20
1934	21	Regisseurin	22	Triumph of the Will	23
1959	24	Schriftsteller	"Die Blechtrommel"	25	Roman
1994	26	27	28	The Lion King	29
1987	Wim Wenders	Regisseur	30	Wings of Desire	31
1998	Franke Potente	32	"Lola rennt"	33	Film

Erweiterung

Double infinitives

In **Kapitel 5**, you learned the past participles of the modal verbs. However, when modal verbs are used with a second verb in the perfect tense, not the past participle but rather a *double infinitive* is used. Compare the following sentence pairs:

Bernd **hat** nach Hause **gemusst.**
Bernd **hat** nach Hause **gehen müssen.** } *Bernd had to go home.*

Das **haben** wir nicht **gekonnt.**
Das **haben** wir nicht **tun können.** } *We couldn't do that.*

The infinitive of the modal verb always follows the infinitive of the other verb. Note that both sentences in each pair use the auxiliary **haben**, as is always the case with modal verbs. In conversational German, speakers often find the double infinitive awkward and instead prefer to substitute the simple past tense:

Bernd **musste** nach Hause **gehen.**　　*Bernd had to go home.*

Das **konnten** wir nicht **tun.**　　*We couldn't do that.*

However, in the past tense subjunctive, whose formation is based on the perfect tense, this alternative to the double infinitive does not exist:

Bernd **hätte** nach Hause **gehen müssen.**　　*Bernd would have had to go home.*

Das **hätten** wir nicht **tun können.**　　*We couldn't have done that.*

As you may have noticed from the above examples, in independent clauses the auxiliary **haben** is inflected and appears in the second position, while the double infinitive is positioned at the end of the sentence. In dependent clauses, however, word order deviates from normal rules:

Bernd ist nicht ins Kino gegangen,
　weil er nach Hause **hat gehen müssen.**
Bernd didn't go to the movies
　because he had to go home.

Sie haben uns gesagt, dass wir
　das nicht **hätten tun können.**
They told us that we couldn't
　have done that.

The auxiliary verb appears not at the end of the dependent clause, as is usually the case, but rather precedes the double infinitive.

12-22 Einen Abend mit den Eltern. Anna and Jörg Christiansen recently spent an evening out with Anna's parents. Rewrite the sentences using the perfect tense.

BEISPIEL: Meine Eltern wollten uns zum Abendessen einladen.
→   Meine Eltern haben uns zum Abendessen einladen wollen.

1. Die Kinder durften nicht mitkommen.

_____

2. Wir mussten eine Babysitterin finden.

_____

3. Meine Eltern konnten sich das teure Restaurant nicht leisten.

_____

4. Mutter sagte uns nicht, dass wir nachher mit ihnen ins Theater gehen kounten.

_____

5. Ich wusste nicht, dass ich meine Brille mitbringen musste.

_____

6. Ich wollte nach Hause, weil ich ohne Brille die Aufführung (*performance*) nicht sehen konnte.

_____

12-23 Was hätte die Babysitterin machen müssen? Good babysitters are hard to find. When the Christiansens return home, everything is in a state of disarray: the children are not in bed and the house is a disaster area. What could or should the babysitter have done differently? Write what she might have done in each of the situations.

BEISPIEL: Es ist den Kindern kalt gewesen.
→   Die Babysitterin hätte eine Decke holen können.
ODER   Sie hätte die Heizung anstellen sollen.

1. Ein Krimi lief im Fernsehen und die Kinder hatten Angst.

_____

2. Die Kinder haben im Haus Basketball gespielt.

_____

3. Der Junge hatte hohes Fieber.

_____

4. Das Mädchen hatte Hunger.

_____

5. Der Freund der Babysitterin ist vorbeigekommen.

_____

6. Die Nachbarn haben wegen des großen Lärms im Haus die Polizei angerufen.

_____

Lab Manual

Kapitel 1

Grüß dich! Ich heiße . . .

Gespräche

1-1 Wie heißt du? Ich heiße. . . Listen carefully to the recorded conversations in **Schritt 1** from your textbook. You may read along in your textbook. If you like, you may replay the dialogues and read aloud along with the recording.

1-2 Woher kommst du? Ich komme aus . . . Listen carefully to the conversations in **Schritt 3**. If you like, you may replay the dialogues and read aloud along with the recording.

1-3 Wie geht's? Es geht mir . . . Listen carefully to the conversations in **Schritt 4**. If you like, you may replay the dialogues and read aloud along with the recording.

1-4 Wie schreibt man das? / Das Alphabet. The German alphabet contains the same twenty-six letters as the English alphabet. Listen carefully and repeat each one after the speaker.

There are also four additional letters. Repeat them after the speaker. Follow along in **Schritt 5** of your book, if you prefer.

1-5 Wie heißen Sie? Listen carefully to the conversations in **Schritt 6.** Then replay them and read aloud along with the recording, if you like.

1-6 Eins, zwei, drei . . . You will recognize many German numbers as having cognates in English. Listen carefully and repeat each number after the speaker. Follow along in **Schritt 7** of your book, if you prefer.

1-7 Wiederholen Sie! You will now hear the conversation from **Schritt 8**. It will be read twice. The first time, just listen. The second time, repeat each phrase during the pause provided.

Aussprache

The *ie*- and *ei*-sounds

The **ie**-sound is pronounced *ee*, as in the girl's name *Marie*. The **ei**-sound is pronounced as in *Eisenhower*.

1-8 Der *ie*-Laut. Now practice the **ie**-sound. Repeat each word after the speaker. Remember: **ie** = *Marie*

vier	sieben	geschrieben	Lieselotte
Riesling	dieser	lieber	schiebt
siebzig	siebzehn	Liebe	Diebe
Friede	Wien	Kiel	

1-9 Der *ei*-Laut. Now practice the **ei**-sound. Repeat each word after the speaker. Remember: **ei** = *Eisenhower*.

eins	zwei	drei	einen
Hein(e)rich	Freiheit	Elfenbein	streiten
Wein	sein	mein	dein
kein	fein	klein	Keil

1-10 *Ei* und *ie*. Now practice these sounds in pairs. Repeat each pair after the speaker.

drei	vier
Wein	Wien
Keil	Kiel
bleiben	blieben
heißen	hießen

1-11 *Ei* oder *ie*? You will hear a series of words. Circle **ei** or **ie** to indicate which sound you hear. You can check your answers with the *Lab Manual Answer Key*.

1. ei	ie		6. ei	ie
2. ei	ie		7. ei	ie
3. ei	ie		8. ei	ie
4. ei	ie		9. ei	ie
5. ei	ie		10. ei	ie

1-12 Versuch's mal! Now you will hear the poem from the **Versuch's mal!** section of your textbook. You will hear the complete poem once; listen carefully, following along in your book if you prefer. You will then hear the poem again, with pauses. Repeat each phrase after the speaker.

1-13 Zungenbrecher (*tongue twister*). You will hear a tongue twister. It will be read twice. The first time, just listen. The second time, repeat each phrase during the pause.

Meine Mutter möchte mit meiner Mieze meine Mäuse mästen.

Strukturen

Subject pronouns

1-14 Pronomen. You will hear a series of statements. Replace the subject of each statement with a pronoun. Then you will hear the correct answer. Repeat the correct answer after the speaker.

BEISPIEL:	YOU HEAR:	Die Frau kommt aus Deutschland.
	YOU SAY:	Sie kommt aus Deutschland.
	YOU HEAR:	Sie kommt aus Deutschland.
	YOU REPEAT:	Sie kommt aus Deutschland.

1. ---   5. ---

2. ---   6. ---

3. ---   7. ---

4. ---   8. ---

The present tense

1-15 Neue Sätze. You will hear a series of statements, each followed by a pronoun. Substitute the pronoun for the subject to form a new sentence. You will then hear the correct answer. Repeat the correct answer.

BEISPIEL:	YOU HEAR:	Ich heiße Peter. (du)
	YOU SAY:	Du heißt Peter.
	YOU HEAR:	Du heißt Peter.
	YOU REPEAT:	Du heißt Peter.

1. ---   4. ---

2. ---   5. ---

3. ---   6. ---

1-16 Verb und Pronomen. You will hear a series of verbs, each followed by a pronoun. Give the correct ending of the verb. You will then hear the correct answer. Repeat the correct answer after the speaker.

BEISPIEL: YOU HEAR: kommen / ich
           YOU SAY: ich komme
           YOU HEAR: ich komme
           YOU REPEAT: ich komme

1. ---   6. ---
2. ---   7. ---
3. ---   8. ---
4. ---   9. ---
5. ---   10. ---

1-17 Ein neues Verb. You will hear a series of statements, each followed by a verb. Substitute the verb in the sentence. You will then hear the correct answer. Repeat the correct answer after the speaker.

BEISPIEL: YOU HEAR: Frau Sommer wohnt in Leipzig. (sein)
           YOU SAY: Frau Sommer ist in Leipzig.
           YOU HEAR: Frau Sommer ist in Leipzig.
           YOU REPEAT: Frau Sommer ist in Leipzig.

1. ---   5. ---
2. ---   6. ---
3. ---   7. ---
4. ---   8. ---

1-18 Singular oder Plural? You will hear a series of statements. Circle **S**, **P**, or *either* to indicate whether each statement is singular or plural, or whether it could be either singular or plural. Each sentence is read twice. You can check your answers with the *Lab Manual Answer Key.*

1. S   P   either   4. S   P   either
2. S   P   either   5. S   P   either
3. S   P   either

1-19 Fragen. You will hear a series of questions. Give a positive answer in a complete sentence. You will then hear the correct answer. Repeat the correct answer after the speaker.

BEISPIEL: YOU HEAR: Du heißt Peter, nicht wahr?
              YOU SAY: Ja, ich heiße Peter.
              YOU HEAR: Ja, ich heiße Peter.
              YOU REPEAT: Ja, ich heiße Peter.

1. ---   4. ---

2. ---   5. ---

3. ---

Hörverständnis

1-20 Diktat: Anrufbeantworter (*answering machine*)**.** You will hear a short paragraph. It will be read once in its entirety, then again with pauses. Use the pauses to write what you have heard. You may replay the recording as often as needed.

_____

_____

_____

_____

_____

_____

1-21 Eine Party. You are planning to give a party with a friend, and she wants to give you some names and phone numbers of people to call and invite. She has left a message on your answering machine. Listen to the message and jot down the numbers you hear. You can check your answers with the *Lab Manual Answer Key*.

Alexandra: _____

Alex: _____

Michelle: _____

Oliver: _____

Was ist Karls Problem? _____

1-22 Ein Gespräch. It is the first day of classes, and a German student is introducing himself to you. He will mention certain facts about himself then ask you questions. Answer in complete sentences. You may stop the recording while you answer aloud.

Kapitel 2

Meine Familie und meine Freunde

Gespräche

2-1 Erikas Familie. Listen carefully to the recorded conversation in **Schritt 5** from your textbook.

2-2 Wiederholen Sie! Now listen again to the conversation and repeat each phrase during the pause provided.

Aussprache

The *ch*-sound

English-speakers need to give special attention to the so-called back **ch** and front **ch**. Listen carefully to the recordings. The back **ch** is produced in the back of the mouth. It is usually preceded by an **a, o, u,** or **au**. The front **ch**, produced in the front of the mouth, is preceded by any letter other than **a, o, u, au,** or **s**. The front **ch** is similar to English *h* in *huge*.

2-3 Der *ach*-Laut. Practice the back **ch** sound. Repeat each word after the speaker.

nach	hoch
auch	kochen
machen	suchen
Sachen	Kuchen

2-4 Der *ich*-Laut. Now practice the front **ch** sound. Repeat each word after the speaker.

nicht	echt
schlecht	lächeln
ich	Köchin
Schwäche	Architekt

When the **ch** is part of the **-chen** suffix, it is pronounced like the front **ch**. Repeat after the speaker.

Mädchen   Hündchen
Liebchen   Häuschen

2-5 *Ach* **oder** *ich*-**Laut?** You will hear a series of words with either the back or front **ch** sound. Repeat each word after the speaker, then circle *back ch* or *front ch* to indicate which sound you heard.

1. back **ch**   front **ch**
2. back **ch**   front **ch**
3. back **ch**   front **ch**
4. back **ch**   front **ch**
5. back **ch**   front **ch**
6. back **ch**   front **ch**

2-6 Die *ch-* **+** *s*-**Laute.** If the **ch** is followed by an **s**, it is pronounced almost like an English *x*. Repeat each word after the speaker.

sechs   Fuchs
Lachs   wachsen

2-7 Versuch's mal! Now you will hear the passage from the **Versuch's mal!** section of your textbook. You will hear the complete passage once; listen carefully, following along in your book if you prefer. You will then hear a portion of it again, with pauses. Repeat each phrase after the speaker.

2-8 Zungenbrecher. You will hear a tongue twister. It will be read twice. The first time, just listen. The second time, repeat each phrase during the pause.

Ach, mach doch endlich einen Kuchen in der Küche!

Strukturen

Nouns

2-9 Pronomen. You will hear a series of statements. Replace the subject of each statement with a pronoun. You will then hear the correct answer. Repeat the correct answer after the speaker.

BEISPIEL: YOU HEAR: Die Telefonnummer ist 38 45 90.
               YOU SAY: Sie ist 38 45 90.
              YOU HEAR: Sie ist 38 45 90.
          YOU REPEAT: Sie ist 38 45 90.

1. ---   3. ---
2. ---   4. ---

2-10 Singular oder Plural? You will hear a series of nouns. Circle **S** or **P** to indicate whether the word is singular or plural.

1. S	P		6. S	P
2. S	P		7. S	P
3. S	P		8. S	P
4. S	P		9. S	P
5. S	P		10. S	P

The nominative case

2-11 Der bestimmte (*definite*) Artikel. You will hear a series of words in the plural. For each one, give the singular form, both noun and article. You will then hear the correct answer. Repeat the correct answer after the speaker.

BEISPIEL: YOU HEAR: Kinder
               YOU SAY: das Kind
             YOU HEAR: das Kind
         YOU REPEAT: das Kind

1. ---   5. ---
2. ---   6. ---
3. ---   7. ---
4. ---   8. ---

2-12 Der unbestimmte (*indefinite*) **Artikel.** You will hear a series of nouns with their definite article. Repeat each noun with its indefinite article. You will then hear the correct answer. Repeat the correct answer after the speaker.

1. ---
2. ---
3. ---
4. ---

5. ---
6. ---
7. ---
8. ---

2-13 Das Subjekt. You will hear a series of statements, each read twice. Say who or what the subject of each sentence is. You will then hear the correct answer.

1. ---
2. ---
3. ---

4. ---
5. ---
6. ---

2-14 Possessive Adjektive. You will hear a series of statements, each followed by a pronoun. Use the pronoun to form a possessive adjective, and insert it into the sentence, replacing the original possessive. You will then hear the correct answer. Repeat the correct answer after the speaker.

BEISPIEL:	YOU HEAR:	Meine Großmutter wohnt in Amerika. (er)
	YOU SAY:	Seine Großmutter wohnt in Amerika.
	YOU HEAR:	Seine Großmutter wohnt in Amerika.
	YOU REPEAT:	Seine Großmutter wohnt in Amerika.

1. ---
2. ---
3. ---

4. ---
5. ---
6. ---

Word order

2-15 Nein . . . ! One student is telling another student about their friends, but he is not always right. After each sentence, you will hear a cue. Use the cue to reply negatively to each statement. You will then hear the correct answer. Repeat the correct answer after the speaker.

BEISPIEL:	YOU HEAR:	Heute geht Hans in die Stadt. (morgen)
	YOU SAY:	Nein, morgen geht Hans in die Stadt.
	YOU HEAR:	Nein, morgen geht Hans in die Stadt.
	YOU REPEAT:	Nein, morgen geht Hans in die Stadt.

1. ---
2. ---

3. ---
4. ---

2-16 *Nicht* oder *kein*. You will hear a series of questions. Answer each one in the negative, using **nicht** or **kein**. You will then hear the correct answer. Repeat the correct answer after the speaker.

1. ---	5. ---
2. ---	6. ---
3. ---	7. ---
4. ---	8. ---

2-17 Richtig oder falsch? You will hear several statements. Correct the sentences that are not true for you by adding **nicht** or **kein**. If the sentence is true for you, simply repeat it after the speaker with **Ja, ...** You will then hear both possible answers.

BEISPIEL: YOU HEAR: Ich koche gern.
              YOU SAY: Nein, ich koche nicht gern.
                 OR: Ja, ich koche gern.

1. ---	5. ---
2. ---	6. ---
3. ---	7. ---
4. ---	8. ---

The verb *haben*

2-18 Hast du Geschwister? Your friend Karl is getting over a head cold and can't hear very well. You will hear a series of statements, each followed by a noun or pronoun. Replace the subject with the new noun or pronoun. You will then hear the correct answer. Repeat the correct response after the speaker.

1. ---	4. ---
2. ---	5. ---
3. ---	6. ---

Hörverständnis

2-19 Diktat: Mein Klassenzimmer. You will hear a short paragraph. It will be read once in its entirety, then again with pauses. Use the pauses to write what you have heard. You may replay the passage as often as needed.

_____

_____

_____

_____

2-20 Familienfotos. Two students, Brigitte and Rolf, are showing each other pictures of their families. Listen to their conversation, then complete the chart. You may replay the dialogue as often as needed.

	NAMEN	BERUFE
Rolfs Geschwister	1.	
	2.	
Brigittes Geschwister	1.	
	2.	
	3.	

Wer ist oft verliebt? _____

verlobt? _____

verheiratet? _____

2-21 Persönliche Fragen. You will hear five questions about yourself and your family. Answer them truthfully, in complete sentences. You may stop the recording as you respond aloud.

1. ---
2. ---
3. ---

4. ---
5. ---

Kapitel 3

Meine Sachen, deine Sachen . . .

Gespräche

3-1 Studenten in Tübingen. Listen carefully to the recorded conversation in **Schritt 4** from the textbook.

3-2 Musst du, oder willst du nur? Listen carefully to the recorded conversation from **Schritt 8** from the textbook.

3-3 Widerholen Sie! Now listen again to the first part of the recorded conversation in **Schritt 8** from the textbook and repeat the phrases during the pause provided.

Aussprache

The *w*-sound

The German *w* sounds like the English *v*.

3-4 Der *w*-Laut. Repeat each word after the speaker.

Wind	wohin
Wasser	weiß
wer	wissen
wollen	was

3-5 *F*- oder *w*-Laut? You will hear a series of words. Decide whether they contain an **f** or a **w** sound and circle the appropriate letter.

1. f	w		6. f	w
2. f	w		7. f	w
3. f	w		8. f	w
4. f	w		9. f	w
5. f	w		10. f	w

3-6 Versuch's mal! Now you will hear a series of tongue twisters from the **Versuch's mal!** section of your textbook. You will hear them twice; the first time, just listen, following along in your book if you prefer. The second time, repeat each phrase after the speaker.

Strukturen

The accusative case

3-7 Wer hat was? You will hear a series of names and objects. For each pair, form a complete sentence using the verb **haben**. You will then hear the correct answer. Repeat the correct answer after the speaker.

BEISPIEL: YOU HEAR: Peter, die Lampe
YOU SAY: Peter hat die Lampe.

1. ---	5. ---
2. ---	6. ---
3. ---	7. ---
4. ---	8. ---

3-8 Was brauchen sie noch? Several students are furnishing their apartment. You will hear a number of items that they might need. Say what each person needs using **brauchen** and the indefinite article. You will then hear the correct answer. Repeat the correct answer after the speaker.

BEISPIEL: YOU HEAR: Hans, das Buch
YOU SAY: Hans braucht ein Buch.

1. ---	4. ---
2. ---	5. ---
3. ---	6. ---

The accusative case / The phrase *es gibt*

3-9 Was gibt es im Zimmer? You will hear a series of items. For each one, say that it is in your room using the phrase **es gibt**. You will then hear the correct answer. Repeat the correct answer after the speaker.

BEISPIEL: YOU HEAR: Bett
YOU SAY: Ja, es gibt ein Bett.

1. ---	5. ---
2. ---	6. ---
3. ---	7. ---
4. ---	8. ---

3-10 Wer braucht wen? You will hear a series of English sentences. Give the German equivalent. You will then hear the correct answer. Repeat the correct answer after the speaker. Use the **du** form for *you,* unless the speaker tells you otherwise.

1. ---   5. ---
2. ---   6. ---
3. ---   7. ---
4. ---

Prepositions with the accusative

3-11 Für Freunde und Familie einkaufen (*shopping*). You will hear a series of names and of items you must buy. For each pair, form a complete sentence. You will then hear the correct answer. Repeat the correct answer after the speaker.

BEISPIEL: YOU HEAR: Mutter, eine Zeitung
                YOU SAY: Für meine Mutter kaufe ich eine Zeitung.

1. ---   5. ---
2. ---   6. ---
3. ---   7. ---
4. ---   8. ---

3-12 *Durch, für, gegen, ohne, um.* You will hear a series of incomplete statements. Each will be read twice. Circle the correct preposition that correctly completes the statement.

1. durch   gegen   für
2. durch   um   gegen
3. ohne   für   gegen
4. durch   für   gegen
5. für   gegen   um
6. durch   ohne   um

The modal verbs *können, müssen, wollen*

The verb form *möchte(n)*

3-13 *Wollen, können, möchten.* You will hear a series of sentences, each followed by a verb. Replace the verb in the sentence with the appropriate form of the new verb. You will then hear the correct answer. Repeat the correct answer after the speaker.

BEISPIEL: YOU HEAR: Die Frau braucht einen Kuli. (wollen)
YOU SAY: Die Frau will einen Kuli.

1. ---
2. ---
3. ---

4. ---
5. ---

3-14 Noch einmal Modalverben. You will hear a series of statements, each followed by a modal verb. Substitute the noun or pronoun to form a new sentence. You will then hear the correct answer. Repeat the correct answer after the speaker.

BEISPIEL: YOU HEAR: Ich kaufe einen Computer. (wollen)
YOU SAY: Ich will einen Computer kaufen.

1. ---
2. ---

3. ---
4. ---

Verbs with stem-vowel changes

3-15 Verbformen. You will hear a series of statements, each followed by a noun or a pronoun. Substitute the noun or pronoun to form a new sentence. You will then hear the correct answer. Repeat the correct answer after the speaker.

BEISPIEL: YOU HEAR: Ich lese gern die Zeitung. (du)
YOU SAY: Du liest gern die Zeitung.

1. ---
2. ---
3. ---
4. ---

5. ---
6. ---
7. ---
8. ---

Hörverständnis

3-16 Diktat: Eine deutsche Studentin. You will hear a short paragraph about a German student. It will be read once in its entirety, then again with pauses. Use the pauses to write what you hear. You many listen as often as needed.

_____

_____

_____

_____

_____

_____

_____

_____

_____

3-17 Was Andreas möchte. You will hear a conversation in which two students, Karin and Andreas, discuss their housing situations. Listen carefully, then complete the chart. You may listen as often as needed.

KARIN HAT	KARIN MÖCHTE	ANDREAS MÖCHTE
_____	_____	_____
_____	_____	_____
_____	_____	_____
_____	_____	_____
_____	_____	_____

3-18 Noch ein Gespräch. You have just run into the German student whom you met earlier on campus. Answer his questions in complete sentences. You may stop the recording while you answer aloud.

Kapitel 4

Tagaus, tagein

Gespräche

4-1 Was machst du am Wochenende? Listen carefully to the recorded conversation in **Schritt 5** from your textbook.

4-2 Wiederholen Sie! Now listen again to the conversation and repeat each phrase during the pause provided.

Aussprache

The *r*-sound

4-3 Der *r*-Laut am Anfang. Practice the letter **r** at the beginning of a syllable or in consonant blends. Repeat each word after the speaker.

richtig	Rita
Rock	Türen
Rose	bringen
Rolf	fahren
Rollschuh	gratulieren

When the German **r** is at the end of a word, it is hardly pronounced at all. It is similar to the British or New England pronunciation of *here*: hee-ah.

4-4 Der *r*-Laut am Ende. Repeat each word after the speaker. Let's begin.

Vater	Mutter
Bruder	Kinder
Schwester	vier
fährt	Tier

4-5 Versuch's mal! Now you will hear the poem from the **Versuch's mal!** section of your textbook. You will hear the complete poem once; listen carefully, following along in your book if you prefer. You will then hear the first two verses again, with pauses. Repeat each phrase after the speaker.

4-6 Zungenbrecher. You will hear a tongue twister. It will be read twice. The first time, just listen. The second time, repeat each phrase during the pause.

Die Katze zerkrazt mit ihrer Tatze die Matratze; die Matratze zerkratzt die Katze mit ihrer Tatze.

Strukturen

Telling time

4-7 Sagen Sie es anders! You will hear a series of time expressions. Change those that are in the twenty-four hour system to the twelve hour system, and vice versa. Repeat the correct answer after the speaker.

BEISPIEL: YOU HEAR: 18 Uhr 32
            YOU SAY: Es ist 6 Uhr 32.

1. ---   4. ---
2. ---   5. ---
3. ---

4-8 Wie spät ist es? You will hear a series of time expressions, each read twice. For each one, circle the time you hear.

BEISPIEL: YOU HEAR: Es ist Viertel nach drei.
               YOU SEE: 3.15   3.45   4.03
               YOU CIRCLE: 3.15

1. 4.40   14.30   14.14   4. 5.20   10.25   4.50
2. 1.10   11.10   10.11   5. 7.30   8.30   9.30
3. 7.00   1.07   17.00   6. 1.04   12.45   12.56

The dative case

4-9 Weihnachten (*Christmas*). What do you plan to give the following people? You will hear a series of questions, each followed by a noun. Use the noun to reply to the question. You will then hear the correct answer. Repeat the correct answer after the speaker.

BEISPIEL: YOU HEAR: Was schenken Sie Ihrem Vater? (einen Kugelschreiber)
YOU SAY: Ich schenke meinem Vater einen Kugelschreiber.

1. ---
2. ---
3. ---
4. ---

5. ---
6. ---
7. ---

4-10 Pronomen. You will hear a series of statements, each read twice. For each one, circle the person or thing to which the pronoun refers.

BEISPIEL: YOU HEAR: Der Rechtsanwalt braucht ihn.
YOU SEE: einen Schreibtisch, ein Poster
YOU CIRCLE: einen Schreibtisch

1. ein Bücherregal   eine Landkarte
2. dem Kind   der Familie
3. den Kindern   ihrem Sohn
4. dem Professor   der Professorin
5. eine Kamera   einen Ball
6. meinem Vater   meiner Mutter
7. den Bleistift   die Hefte

4-11 Geburtstag. You will hear a series of questions. Answer them positively, using pronouns instead of nouns. You will then hear the correct answer. Repeat the correct answer after the speaker.

BEISPIEL: YOU HEAR: Geben Sie Ihrem Vater das Heft?
YOU SAY: Ja, ich gebe es ihm.

1. ---
2. ---
3. ---

4. ---
5. ---
6. ---

Dative verbs

4-12 Wem? You will hear a series of questions. Answer each one, using the cue provided. You will then hear the correct answer. Repeat the correct answer after the speaker.

BEISPIEL: YOU HEAR: Wem gehört das Buch? (ihre Schwester)
YOU SAY: Das Buch gehört ihrer Schwester.

1. ---   5. ---
2. ---   6. ---
3. ---   7. ---
4. ---

Prepositions with the dative

4-13 Woher? Wohin? Wo? You will hear a series of statements with prepositional objects, followed by a new noun. Substitute the noun in the prepositional phrase. You will then hear the correct answer. Repeat the correct answer after the speaker.

BEISPIEL: YOU HEAR: Ich komme aus der Schule. (das Haus)
YOU SAY: Ich komme aus dem Haus.

1. ---   4. ---
2. ---   5. ---
3. ---

More time expressions

4-14 Wann machen Sie das? You will hear several pairs of phrases. Combine them into one sentence, using **am** or **im**. You will then hear the correct answer. Repeat the correct answer after the speaker.

BEISPIEL: YOU HEAR: Wochenende, Hausaufgaben machen
YOU SAY: Am Wochenende mache ich Hausaufgaben.

1. ---   4. ---
2. ---   5. ---
3. ---   6. ---

4-15 Persönliche Fragen. You will hear six questions about yourself. Answer them in complete sentences using the proper phrases with **im** (with months and seasons), **am** (with days), or **um** (with times). You may stop the recording as you respond.

1. ---   4. ---
2. ---   5. ---
3. ---   6. ---

Coordinating conjunctions

4-16 Die Jahreszeiten. You will hear several pairs of statements, each read twice. Each pair will be followed by a conjunction. Use the conjunction to combine the sentences. You will then hear the correct answer. Repeat the correct answer after the speaker.

1. ---   4. ---
2. ---   5. ---
3. ---

4-17 *Und, aber, oder, sondern, denn.* You will hear several pairs of statements. Each pair will be read twice. Combine the two statements using a conjunction. You will then hear the appropriate answer. Repeat it after the speaker.

1. ---   4. ---
2. ---   5. ---
3. ---

The simple past of *sein*

4-18 Ich war, du warst... You will hear a series of questions, each followed by a pronoun. Substitute the pronoun into the sentence. You will then hear the correct answer. Repeat the correct answer after the speaker.

BEISPIEL: YOU HEAR: Wo war er diese Woche? (du)
                 YOU SAY: Wo warst du diese Woche?

1. ---   4. ---
2. ---   5. ---
3. ---   6. ---

Hörverständnis

4-19 Diktat: Eriks Ferien. You will hear a short paragraph about Erik and Susie. It will be read once in its entirety, then again with pauses. Use the pauses to write what you have heard. You may listen as often as needed.

_____

_____

_____

_____

_____

_____

_____

4-20 Gespräch. You will hear a conversation in which two young people, Petra and Dieter, discuss their friend's birthday. Listen carefully, then answer the questions. You may listen to the dialogue as often as needed.

FRAGEN:

1. Wer hat Geburtstag? _____

2. Wann hat er Geburtstag? _____

3. Was macht Klaus gern? _____

4. Was schenken ihm Petra und Dieter? _____

Kapitel 5

Wie und wo wohnen wir?

Gespräche

5-1 Meine Mitbewohnerin ist ausgezogen. Listen carefully to the recorded conversation in **Schritt 7** from your textbook.

5-2 Michelle und Tom kaufen zusammen ein. Listen carefully to the recorded conversation in **Schritt 9** from your textbook.

5-3 Wiederholen Sie! Now listen again to the first part of the conversation in **Schritt 9**, and repeat each phrase during the pause provided.

Aussprache

The *z*-sound

In German, the final and initial **z** are pronounces like a *ts* in the English word *cats*. In English words, this sound occurs only at the end of a syllable. In German, this sound occurs at the beginning, in the middle and also at the end of a word.

5-4 Der *z*-Laut. Repeat each word after the speaker.

Zoo	Salz
Zaun	Zahn
Zug	Zeit
ziehen	Zone
Kreuz	Wurzel
ganz	zu
Wohnzimmer	Heizung

5-5 Versuch's mal! Now you will hear the passage from the **Versuch's mal!** section of your textbook. You will hear the complete passage once; listen carefully, following along in your book if you prefer. You will then hear a portion of it again with pauses. Repeat each phrase after the speaker.

Strukturen

The modal verbs *dürfen, sollen, mögen* and summary of all modals

5-6 Was darf sein? You will hear a series of sentences, each followed by a modal verb. Substitute the modal verb into the sentence. You will then hear the correct answer. Repeat the correct answer after the speaker.

BEISPIEL: YOU HEAR: Die Lehrerin kann nicht viel sagen. (wollen)
YOU SAY: Die Lehrerin will nicht viel sagen.

1. ---
2. ---
3. ---
4. ---
5. ---
6. ---

5-7 Noch mehr Modalverben. You will hear a series of sentences, each followed by a modal verb. Insert the modal verb into the sentence. You will then hear the correct answer. Repeat the correct answer after the speaker.

BEISPIEL: YOU HEAR: Bert mietet eine Wohnung. (sollen)
YOU SAY: Bert soll eine Wohnung mieten.

1. ---
2. ---
3. ---
4. ---
5. ---
6. ---

wissen / kennen / können

5-8 *wissen, kennen, können.* You will hear a series of questions, each followed by a verb. Use that verb to form a new question. You will then hear the correct answer. Repeat the correct answer after the speaker.

BEISPIEL: YOU HEAR: Willst du schnell laufen? (können)
YOU SAY: Kannst du schnell laufen?

1. ---
2. ---
3. ---
4. ---
5. ---
6. ---
7. ---
8. ---

5-9 *Wissen* oder *kennen*? You will hear a series of incomplete statements; each will be read twice. Circle the verb that would best complete the statement.

1. kenne   weiß
2. kennen   wissen
3. kennst   weißt
4. kennt   weiß
5. kenne   weiß

The present perfect tense

5-10 Heute bin ich faul! You will hear a series of questions asking whether you plan to complete various activities today. Reply that you did them yesterday. You will then hear the correct answer. Repeat the correct answer after the speaker.

BEISPIEL: YOU HEAR: Lernst du viel?
            YOU SAY: Nein, gestern habe ich viel gelernt.

1. ---   5. ---
2. ---   6. ---
3. ---   7. ---
4. ---   8. ---

5-11 Letzten Samstag. You will hear a series of verbs, followed by incomplete sentences about the activities of various people last Saturday. Use the verb to complete the sentences. You will then hear the correct answer. Repeat the correct answer after the speaker.

BEISPIEL: YOU HEAR: sehen: Meine Tante hat mich . . .
            YOU SAY: Meine Tante hat mich gesehen.

1. ---   5. ---
2. ---   6. ---
3. ---   7. ---
4. ---   8. ---

5-12 Letzte Woche. You will hear a series of phrases. Say that you did each activity last week. You will then hear the correct answer. Repeat the correct answer after the speaker.

BEISPIEL: YOU HEAR: nicht viel schlafen
            YOU SAY: Letzte Woche habe ich nicht viel geschlafen.

1. ---   6. ---
2. ---   7. ---
3. ---   8. ---
4. ---   9. ---
5. ---   10. ---

Separable and inseparable prefix verbs

5-13 Was wir machen. Several students are telling each other what their friends do. You will hear a series of names, each followed by a verb. Form a complete sentence, saying that the person likes to do the activity mentioned. You will then hear the correct answer. Repeat the correct answer after the speaker.

BEISPIEL: YOU HEAR: Susan, fernsehen
YOU SAY: Susan sieht gern fern.

1. ---   3. ---
2. ---   4. ---

5-14 Fragen. You will hear a series of phrases. Form questions in the **Sie**-form in the present tense. You will then hear the correct answer. Repeat the correct answer after the speaker.

BEISPIEL: YOU HEAR: mitkommen
YOU SAY: Kommen Sie mit?

1. ---   5. ---
2. ---   6. ---
3. ---   7. ---
4. ---   8. ---

5-15 Trennbar oder untrennbar? You will hear a series of sentences in the present perfect tense. If you hear a **ge-** prefix in the past participle, circle **S** for *separable prefix*. If you did not hear a **ge-** prefix, circle **I** for *inseparable prefix*.

1. S   I   5. S   I
2. S   I   6. S   I
3. S   I   7. S   I
4. S   I   8. S   I

5-16 Was ist passiert? You will hear a series of sentences, each followed by a verb. Substitute the verb into the sentence. You will then hear the correct answer. Repeat the correct answer after the speaker.

1. ---   5. ---
2. ---   6. ---
3. ---   7. ---
4. ---   8. ---

Hörverständnis

5-17 Diktat: Franks Wohnung. You will hear a short paragraph. It will be read once in its entirety, then again with pauses. Use the pauses to write what you have heard. You may replay the passage as often as needed.

_____

_____

_____

_____

_____

_____

_____

_____

_____

5-18 Ein Brief. You will hear a letter to Oliver; the letter was written by his friend who is studying in Germany. Listen carefully, then read the incomplete sentences in your *Lab Manual*. Circle the letter of the word or words that correctly complete the sentences. Some sentences may have more than one correct answer.

1. John studiert in . . .
   a. Berlin
   b. Heidelberg
   c. Mannheim

2. Die Wohnung hat . . .
   a. eine Küche
   b. kein Esszimmer
   c. drei Schlafzimmer

3. Die Studenten . . .
   a. kochen zusammen
   b. sehen zusammen fern
   c. reisen zusammen

5-19 Persönliche Fragen. You will hear five questions about yourself. Answer them in complete sentences. You may pause the recording as you respond.

1. ---
2. ---
3. ---

4. ---
5. ---

Kapitel 6

Gesundheit und Körper

Gespräche

6-1 Ein Besuch bei der Ärztin. Listen carefully to the recorded conversation in **Schritt 7** from your textbook.

6-2 Wiederholen Sie! Now listen again to the first part of the conversation and repeat each phrase during the pause provided.

Aussprache

The *s* + consonant sound

The **s** in German is sometimes pronounced differently when used in conjunction with other consonants than when it is used alone. For instance, the combinations **st** and **sp**, when they appear at the beginning of a word or syllable, are pronounced like the English *sh* plus *p* or *t*, respectively.

If these combinations are located anywhere else in the word, they are pronounced as in English.

6-3 Der *s* + Konsonant-Laut. Repeat each word after the speaker.

spielen	sprechen
besprechen	Stück
bestellen	Straße
Stunde	Sport
Obst	erst
kosten	Osten
Westen	Herbst
beste	hast

6-4 Versuch's mal! Now you will hear the passage from the **Versuch's mal!** section of your textbook. You will hear the complete passage once; listen carefully, following along in your textbook if you prefer. You will then hear the portion again, with pauses. Repeat each phrase after the speaker.

6-5 Zungenbrecher. You will hear a tongue twister. It will be read twice. The first time, just listen. The second time, repeat each phrase during the pause.

Stolpern Sie nicht über einen spitzen Stein!

Strukturen

Expressions of time with adverbs

6-6 Wie oft tun Sie das? You will hear a series of activities. Using complete sentences, say when you do these things. Use adverbs such as **täglich**, **oft**, **morgens**, **manchmal**, **übermorgen**, and so on. You may stop the recording as you respond.

1. ---
2. ---
3. ---
4. ---

5. ---
6. ---
7. ---
8. ---

Adjective endings

6-7 In der Mensa. Irene and Karin are chatting in the cafeteria. You will hear a series of sentences, each followed by an adjective. Insert the adjective into the sentence before the noun. You will then hear the correct answer. Repeat the correct answer after the speaker.

BEISPIEL: YOU HEAR: Der Student heißt Peter. (groß)
            YOU SAY: Der große Student heißt Peter.

1. ---
2. ---
3. ---
4. ---
5. ---

6. ---
7. ---
8. ---
9. ---
10. ---

6-8 Der Körper. You will hear a series of sentences with predicate adjectives. Change them to sentences with attributive adjectives. You will then hear the correct answer. Repeat the correct answer after the speaker.

BEISPIEL: YOU HEAR: Meine Nase ist rot.
            YOU SAY: Ich habe eine rote Nase.

1. ---
2. ---
3. ---
4. ---

5. ---
6. ---
7. ---
8. ---

6-9 Was kauft Marc? It's Marc's first semester at the university, and he is shopping for his supplies. You will hear a series of his statements, each followed by an adjective. Insert the adjective into the sentence before the noun. You will then hear the correct answer. Repeat the correct answer after the speaker.

BEISPIEL: YOU HEAR: Ich brauche die Hefte. (blau)
YOU SAY: Ich brauche die blauen Hefte.

1. ---
2. ---
3. ---
4. ---
5. ---

6. ---
7. ---
8. ---
9. ---
10. ---

Reflexive verbs

6-10 Was man jeden Tag tut. You will hear a series of sentences, each followed by a pronoun. Substitute the pronoun into the sentence. You will then hear the correct answer. Repeat the correct answer after the speaker.

BEISPIEL: YOU HEAR: Ich muss mich zuerst waschen. (er)
YOU SAY: Er muss sich zuerst waschen.

1. ---
2. ---
3. ---
4. ---
5. ---

6. ---
7. ---
8. ---
9. ---
10. ---

6-11 Fragen. You are walking across campus and run into a German acquaintance. Answer his questions in complete sentences. You may pause or stop the recording as you respond.

1. ---
2. ---
3. ---

4. ---
5. ---

Hörverständnis

6-12 Diktat: Gesund leben. You will hear a short paragraph. It will be read once in its entirety, then again with pauses. Use the pauses to write what you have heard. You may listen as often as needed.

_____

_____

_____

_____

_____

_____

_____

_____

_____

_____

6-13 Logisch oder unlogisch. You will hear a series of statements, each read twice. Circle **L** if the sentence is logical, **U** if the sentence is not.

1. L   U   6. L   U
2. L   U   7. L   U
3. L   U   8. L   U
4. L   U   9. L   U
5. L   U   10. L   U

6-14 Gesundheit ist wichtig. You will hear a brief passage as Thomas, a student, talks about his health. Listen carefully, then decide whether the following statements are true (**richtig**) or false (**falsch**), based on the passage. You may listen to the recording as often as needed.

1. Thomas ist nicht fit.	richtig	falsch
2. Thomas muss schwer arbeiten.	richtig	falsch
3. Er ernährt sich gut.	richtig	falsch
4. Er joggt zweimal pro Woche.	richtig	falsch
5. Er hat nicht viel Zeit zur Entspannung.	richtig	falsch
6. Thomas geht gern zum Arzt.	richtig	falsch

Kapitel 7

Lass uns etwas zusammen unternehmen!

Gespräche

7-1 Machen wir etwas zusammen? Listen carefully to the recorded conversation in **Schritt 4** from your textbook.

7-2 Wiederholen Sie! Now listen again to the first half of the conversation and repeat each phrase during the pause provided.

Aussprache

The *ä*-sound

The German long **ä**-sound is similar to the English vowel in *made*. The short **ä** is like the German short **e**; it resembles the English vowel sound in *rent*.

7-3 Der lange *ä*-Laut. Repeat each word after the speaker.

später	Käse
zählen	hämisch
Gräser	mäßig
Väter	

7-4 Der kurze *ä*-Laut. Repeat each word after the speaker.

Stätte	fällen
Plätze	lässig
hässlich	Äste

7-5 Versuch's mal! Now you will hear the poem from the **Versuch's mal!** section of your textbook. You will hear the complete poem once; listen carefully, following along in your book if you prefer. You will then hear the first verse again, with pauses. Repeat each phrase after the speaker.

Strukturen

Destination vs. location: Two-way prepositions

7-6 Manfreds Zimmer. You will hear a series of questions based on the drawing of Manfred's room below. Each question will be followed by a noun. Answer the questions in complete sentences using the correct prepositions and articles. You will then hear the correct answer. Repeat the correct answer after the speaker.

BEISPIEL: YOU HEAR: Wo ist das Handy? (der Rucksack)
YOU SAY: Das Handy ist in dem Rucksack.

1. ---
2. ---
3. ---
4. ---

5. ---
6. ---
7. ---

7-7 Wo sind sie alle? You will hear a series of questions, each followed by a verb. Answer each question negatively, using the new verb. You will then hear the correct answer. Repeat the correct answer after the speaker.

BEISPIEL: YOU HEAR: Geht die Mutter in den Garten? (arbeiten)
YOU SAY: Nein, die Mutter arbeitet in dem Garten.

1. ---
2. ---
3. ---

4. ---
5. ---
6. ---

7-8 Wir sind neu in der Stadt. You will hear a series of questions, followed by a preposition and a noun. The preposition and noun cues are also printed below. Use the cues to answer each question using a prepositional phrase. You will then hear the correct answer. Repeat the correct answer after the speaker.

BEISPIEL: YOU HEAR: Wo steht der Bus? (vor, die Bank)
YOU SAY: Der Bus steht vor der Bank.

1. in / das Museum
2. in / die Altstadt
3. zwischen / die Post, die Kirche
4. vor / der Bahnhof
5. an / die Bushaltestelle
6. an / die Ampel
7. über / die Brücke
8. vor / das Krankenhaus

7-9 Was haben Sie gesagt? You will hear a series of statements. Request that the speaker repeat the information by asking a question with **wo** or **wohin**? In your questions, use **Sie** for *you*. You will then hear the correct answer. Repeat the correct answer after the speaker.

BEISPIEL: YOU HEAR: Ich fahre nach München.
YOU SAY: Wohin fahren Sie?

1. ---   4. ---
2. ---   5. ---
3. ---   6. ---

Command forms

7-10 Auf der Reise. Imagine that you are a chaperone on a senior class trip to Germany. Give the appropriate commands, using the cues you hear. You will then hear the correct answer. Repeat the correct answer after the speaker.

BEISPIEL: YOU HEAR: Andy, hier aussteigen
YOU SAY: Andy, steig hier aus!

1. ---   6. ---
2. ---   7. ---
3. ---   8. ---
4. ---   9. ---
5. ---   10. ---

Ordinal numbers

7-11 Wie viele? You will hear a series of sentences, each followed by an ordinal number. Insert the number into the sentence. You will then hear the correct answer. Repeat the correct answer after the speaker.

BEISPIEL: YOU HEAR: Das ist mein Buch. (zwei)
YOU SAY: Das ist mein zweites Buch.

1. ---
2. ---
3. ---

4. ---
5. ---
6. ---

7-12 Persönliche Fragen. You will hear five personal questions. Answer them in complete sentences. You may stop the recording as you respond.

1. ---
2. ---
3. ---

4. ---
5. ---

Hörverständnis

7-13 Diktat: Heidelberg. You will hear a short paragraph. It will be read once in its entirety, then again with pauses. Use the pauses to write what you have heard. You may listen to the passage as often as needed.

_____

_____

_____

_____

_____

_____

_____

_____

_____

7-14 Entschuldigen Sie, bitte. Wie komme ich nach Lübeck? Lübeck is a city of 215,000 inhabitants in the northern German state of Schleswig-Holstein. You arrive at the tourist information center in Hamburg and ask for directions and some information about the city. Listen carefully and answer the questions. You may listen to the recording as often as needed.

<u>NEUE VOKABELN</u>

der Turm – *tower, steeple*
das Tor – *city gate*

1. Wie lange dauert die Bahnreise von Hamburg nach Lübeck?

   _____

2. Wie viele Kirchen und Dome hat die Lübecker Innenstadt?

   _____

3. Welche Funktion hat heute das Holstentor?

   _____

4. Wo ist das Rathaus?

   _____

5. Was findet man in der Breiten Straße?

   _____

Kapitel 8

Ja gerne, aber . . .

Gespräche

8-1 Kann ich Ihnen helfen? Listen carefully to the recorded conversation from **Schritt 2** of your textbook.

8-2 Becker, guten Tag! Listen carefully to the recorded conversations from **Schritt 4** of your textbook.

8-3 Ein erfolgreiches Gespräch. Listen carefully to the recorded conversations from **Schritt 5** of your textbook.

8-4 Ein Anruf nach Amerika. Listen carefully to the conversation between Judy and her mother in **Schritt 7** of your textbook.

8-5 Wiederholen Sie! Now listen again to the conversation from **Schritt 7** and repeat each phrase during the pause provided.

Aussprache

The *ü*-sound

To pronounce the German **ü**, keep your tongue in the same position as for *ee* (as in *weed*), but round your lips as for long **u**.

8-6 Der *ü*-Laut. Repeat each word after the speaker.

LONG *ü*	SHORT *ü*
Dünen	dünn
berühmt	verrückt
Gemüse	schüchtern
Füße	Schüsse
Mühle	Müll
Stühle	Zahnbürste
Züge	Rücken

8-7 Versuch's mal! Now you will hear a completed version of the advertisement from the **Versuch's mal!** section of your textbook. You will hear it twice; the first time, just listen. The second time, repeat each phrase after the speaker.

The *ö*-sound

To pronounce the German **ö**, keep your tongue in the same position as for the *a* in English *ace*, but round your lips as for long **o**.

8-8 Der *ö*-Laut. Repeat each word after the speaker.

LONG Ö	SHORT Ö
König	können
Höhle	Hölle
schön	schöpfen
Öfen	öffnen
möglich	Mörder
Löhne	Löffel

8-9 Versuch's mal! Now you will hear the three sentences with the **ö**-sound from the **Versuch's mal!** section of your textbook. You will hear it twice; the first time, just listen, following along in your book if you prefer. The second time, repeat each phrase after the speaker.

8-10 *ä*, *ö* oder *ü*? You will hear a series of words. Listen carefully, and repeat each one after the speaker. Then circle **ä**, **ö**, or **ü** according to the sound the word contains.

1. ä	ö	ü	10. ä	ö	ü
2. ä	ö	ü	11. ä	ö	ü
3. ä	ö	ü	12. ä	ö	ü
4. ä	ö	ü	13. ä	ö	ü
5. ä	ö	ü	14. ä	ö	ü
6. ä	ö	ü	15. ä	ö	ü
7. ä	ö	ü	16. ä	ö	ü
8. ä	ö	ü	17. ä	ö	ü
9. ä	ö	ü	18. ä	ö	ü

Strukturen

The *würde* construction

8-11 Was würden wir tun? You and your friends are considering studying in Germany and are discussing what you would do if you were to spend a year there. You will hear a series of cues. Use the cues and the correct form of **würde** to indicate what the people would do. Repeat the correct answer after the speaker.

BEISPIEL: YOU HEAR: Henry, oft nach Amerika telefonieren
             YOU SAY: Henry würde oft nach Amerika telefonieren.

1. ---   4. ---
2. ---   5. ---
3. ---   6. ---

Subordinating conjunctions

8-12 Konjunktionen. You will hear a series of sentence pairs, each followed by a subordinating conjunction. Each pair will be read twice. Combine them into a single sentence using the specified conjunction. You will then hear the correct answer. Repeat the correct answer after the speaker.

BEISPIEL: YOU HEAR: Sebastian will einen Mantel. Es ist ihm kalt.
                        Sebastian will einen Mantel. Es ist ihm kalt. (weil)
             YOU SAY: Sebastian will einen Mantel, weil es ihm kalt ist.

1. ---   5. ---
2. ---   6. ---
3. ---   7. ---
4. ---   8. ---

8-13 Aus zwei mach eins. You will hear a series of sentence pairs, each followed by a subordinating conjunction. Each pair will be read twice. Combine them into a single sentence, this time placing the conjunction at the beginning of the sentence. You will then hear the correct answer. Repeat the correct answer after the speaker.

BEISPIEL: YOU HEAR: Ich brauche eine Hose. Ich gehe einkaufen.
                        Ich brauche eine Hose. Ich gehe einkaufen. (wenn)
             YOU SAY: Wenn ich eine Hose brauche, gehe ich einkaufen.

1. ---   4. ---
2. ---   5. ---
3. ---   6. ---

8-14 Was ist hier logisch? You will hear a series of incomplete sentences. Complete each sentence in a logical way. You may stop the recording as you respond.

1. ---
2. ---
3. ---
4. ---
5. ---

Word order: time–manner–place

8-15 Neue Sätze. You will hear a series of statements, each followed by an adverbial phrase. Each statement will be read twice. Insert the phrase into the sentence. You will then hear the correct answer. Repeat the correct answer after the speaker.

BEISPIEL: YOU HEAR: Wir wollen um 8 Uhr Tennis spielen. (morgen früh)
                              Wir wollen um 8 Uhr Tennis spielen. (morgen früh)
             YOU SAY: Wir wollen morgen früh um 8 Uhr Tennis spielen.

1. ---
2. ---
3. ---
4. ---
5. ---
6. ---
7. ---
8. ---

der- and *ein-*words

8-16 Eine Reise planen. One student is planning a trip and another asks what she is taking with her. Answer her questions using the cues. You will then hear the correct answer. Repeat the correct answer after the speaker.

BEISPIEL: YOU HEAR: Welche Jacke nimmst du mit? (dies-)
             YOU SAY: Ich nehme diese Jacke mit.

1. ---
2. ---
3. ---
4. ---
5. ---
6. ---
7. ---

Hörverständnis

8-17 *Richtig* oder *falsch*? You will hear a series of statements. Circle **R** if they are true, **F** if they are not.

1. R   F   5. R   F
2. R   F   6. R   F
3. R   F   7. R   F
4. R   F

8-18 Ein Telefongespräch. You will hear a telephone conversation between Völker Geller and his friend Anke Stauffer. Listen carefully, then answer the questions. You may replay the conversation as often as needed.

1. Warum ruft Anke ihren Freund Völker an?

   _____

2. Wie viel Geld bekommt Völker monatlich von seinen Eltern?

   _____

3. Was hat er diesen Monat mit dem Geld gemacht?

   _____

4. Welche Vorschläge hat Anke?

   _____

5. Kann Völker mit Anke und Ulrike ausgehen? Warum oder warum nicht?

   _____

Kapitel 9

Guten Appetit!

Gespräche

9-1 Zum Mittagessen im Restaurant *Schöne Aussicht*. Listen carefully to the recorded conversation in **Schritt 6** from your textbook.

9-2 Der Imbiss. Listen carefully to the recorded conversation in **Schritt 8** from your textbook.

9-3 Wiederholen Sie! Now listen again to the first part of the conversation from **Schritt 8** and repeat each phrase during the pauses.

Aussprache

The *kn-* and *pf*-sounds

In German, both consonants are pronounced in the **kn** and **pf** combinations.

9-4 Der *kn*-Laut. Repeat each word after the speaker. Let's begin.

Knopf	Knabe
knicken	knurren
Knoblauch	knusprig
Knie	Knochen

9-5 Der *pf*-Laut. Repeat each word after the speaker.

Pflaume	Apfel
pfeifen	Topf
Pfanne	Pfirsich
Pfeffer	Pflicht

9-6 *Pf* **oder** *ff*? You will hear a series of words. Circle **pf** or **ff** to indicate which sound you hear.

1. pf	ff		6. pf	ff
2. pf	ff		7. pf	ff
3. pf	ff		8. pf	ff
4. pf	ff		9. pf	ff
5. pf	ff		10. pf	ff

9-7 *Kn* **oder** *k*? You will hear a series of words. Circle **kn** or **k** to indicate which sound you hear.

1. kn	k		6. kn	k
2. kn	k		7. kn	k
3. kn	k		8. kn	k
4. kn	k		9. kn	k
5. kn	k		10. kn	k

9-8 Versuch's mal! You will now hear the passage from the **Versuch's mal!** section of your textbook. You will hear the complete passage once; listen carefully, following along in your book if you prefer. You will then hear the passage again, with pauses. Repeat each phrase after the speaker.

Strukturen

Adjective endings

9-9 Was bestellen sie? A group of students are trying a new restaurant in town. What does each person order? You will hear a series of questions, each followed by an adjective and a noun. Use the adjective and noun cues to reply to the question. You will then hear the correct answer. Repeat the correct answer after the speaker.

BEISPIEL: YOU HEAR: Was isst Stefan? (das Rindfleisch, zart)
YOU SAY: Stefan isst das zarte Rindfleisch.

1. ---		6. ---
2. ---		7. ---
3. ---		8. ---
4. ---		9. ---
5. ---		10. ---

9-10 Was mögen sie? You will hear a series of questions. Each will be followed by a noun and an adjective. Use the adjective and noun cues to reply to the question. You will then hear the correct answer. Repeat the correct answer after the speaker.

BEISPIEL: YOU HEAR: Was mag Stefan? (Brot, weiß)
　　　　　　　 YOU SAY: Stefan mag weißes Brot.

1. ---　　　　　　　　　　　　　4. ---
2. ---　　　　　　　　　　　　　5. ---
3. ---　　　　　　　　　　　　　6. ---

9-11 Was schmeckt Lars überhaupt? Lars is a finicky eater. You will hear a noun and an adjective. Use the cues to say what Lars doesn't like. You will then hear the correct answer. Repeat the correct answer after the speaker.

BEISPIEL: YOU HEAR: Eier, gekocht
　　　　　　　 YOU SAY: Gekochte Eier schmecken ihm nicht.

1. ---　　　　　　　　　　　　　5. ---
2. ---　　　　　　　　　　　　　6. ---
3. ---　　　　　　　　　　　　　7. ---
4. ---　　　　　　　　　　　　　8. ---

9-12 Persönliche Fragen. You will hear eight questions about yourself. Answer them in complete sentences. You may stop the recording as you respond.

1. ---　　　　　　　　　　　　　5. ---
2. ---　　　　　　　　　　　　　6. ---
3. ---　　　　　　　　　　　　　7. ---
4. ---　　　　　　　　　　　　　8. ---

Comparative and superlative forms of adjectives and adverbs

9-13 Vergleiche. You will hear a series of sentences comparing equal items. Change them to unequal comparisons with **als**. You will then hear the correct answer. Repeat the correct answer after the speaker.

BEISPIEL: YOU HEAR: Die Zitronen sind **so sauer wie** die Orangen.
　　　　　　　 YOU SAY: Die Zitronen sind **saurer als** die Orangen

1. ---　　　　　　　　　　　　　6. ---
2. ---　　　　　　　　　　　　　7. ---
3. ---　　　　　　　　　　　　　8. ---
4. ---　　　　　　　　　　　　　9. ---
5. ---　　　　　　　　　　　　　10. ---

9-14 Was ist besser? Your German friend is testing your culinary knowledge. Answer his questions in complete sentences. You will then hear the correct answer. Repeat the correct answer after the speaker.

BEISPIEL: YOU HEAR: Welches Gewürz ist schärfer: Pfeffer oder Salz?
                YOU SAY: Pfeffer ist das schärfere Gewürz.

1. ---   5. ---
2. ---   6. ---
3. ---   7. ---
4. ---   8. ---

9-15 Was ist am besten? You will hear a series of sentences comparing unequal items. Each will be followed by a cue. Use the cue to form a new sentence in the superlative. You will then hear the correct answer. Repeat the correct answer after the speaker.

BEISPIEL: YOU HEAR: Kirschen sind weicher als Äpfel. (Pfirsiche)
                YOU SAY: Aber Pfirsiche sind am weichsten.

1. ---   5. ---
2. ---   6. ---
3. ---   7. ---
4. ---   8. ---

9-16 Wer kann das glauben? Helena tends to be an extremist. You will hear a series of sentences, each followed by an adjective. Insert the adjective into the sentence, using the superlative form. You will then hear the correct answer. Repeat the correct answer after the speaker.

BEISPIEL: YOU HEAR: Sie isst in den Restaurants. (teuer)
                YOU SAY: Sie isst in den teuersten Restaurants.

1. ---   5. ---
2. ---   6. ---
3. ---   7. ---
4. ---   8. ---

Demonstrative pronouns

9-17 Hilfe. Your friend forgot his glasses and is asking you questions because he can't see very well. Answer his questions, using the appropriate demonstrative pronoun. You will then hear the correct answer. Repeat the correct answer after the speaker.

BEISPIEL: YOU HEAR: Ist die Ampel grün?
YOU SAY: Ja, die ist grün.

1. ---   4. ---
2. ---   5. ---
3. ---   6. ---

Hörverständnis

9-18 In der Gaststätte. Lisa and Nathan are having lunch at a restaurant in the city. You will hear a brief conversation as they order their food. Listen carefully, then mark below which foods each person has ordered. You may listen to the recording as often as needed.

	LISA	NATHAN
Salat	_____	_____
Kartoffeln	_____	_____
Pommes	_____	_____
Nudeln	_____	_____
Fisch	_____	_____
Hähnchen	_____	_____
Schweinefleisch	_____	_____
grüne Bohnen	_____	_____
Zwiebeln	_____	_____
Mineralwasser	_____	_____
Bier	_____	_____
Zitronensaft	_____	_____

Kapitel 10

Unterwegs

Gespräche

10-1 Vor der Reise. Listen carefully to the recorded conversation from **Schritt 3** of your textbook.

10-2 Wo kann man übernachten? Listen carefully to the recorded conversation from **Schritt 5** of your textbook.

10-3 Am Bahnhof. Listen carefully to the recorded conversation from **Schritt 8** of your textbook.

10-4 Wiederholen Sie! Now listen again to the first part of the conversation from **Schritt 8** and repeat each phrase during the pause provided.

Aussprache

10-5 *Ei* oder *ie*? You will hear a series of words. Repeat each one after the speaker, then circle which sound you heard.

1. ei	ie		6. ei	ie
2. ei	ie		7. ei	ie
3. ei	ie		8. ei	ie
4. ei	ie		9. ei	ie
5. ei	ie		10. ei	ie

10-6 Front *ch* or back *ch*? You will hear a series of words. Repeat each one after the speaker, then circle which sound you heard.

1. front **ch**	back **ch**		6. front **ch**	back **ch**
2. front **ch**	back **ch**		7. front **ch**	back **ch**
3. front **ch**	back **ch**		8. front **ch**	back **ch**
4. front **ch**	back **ch**		9. front **ch**	back **ch**
5. front **ch**	back **ch**		10. front **ch**	back **ch**

10-7 *W* oder *v*? You will hear a series of words. Repeat each one after the speaker, then circle which sound you heard.

1. w	v		6. w	v
2. w	v		7. w	v
3. w	v		8. w	v
4. w	v		9. w	v
5. w	v		10. w	v

10-8 Zungenbrecher. You will hear three tongue twisters. They will be read twice. The first time, just listen. The second time, repeat each phrase during the pause.

Wir verkaufen viel Wein aus Wien und verschiedene Weißbiere aus der Schweiz.

Das Wetter wird vor Mittwochnachmittag vielleicht noch wolkig.

Zum Nachtisch mache ich einen leichten Kuchen mit Pfirsichen.

Strukturen

Infinitives with and without *zu*

10-9 Wie finden Sie das? You will hear a series of sentence pairs. Combine them into a single statement using an infinitive construction with **zu**.

BEISPIEL: YOU HEAR: Ich lerne Deutsch. Ich finde es leicht.
YOU SAY: Ich finde es leicht, Deutsch zu lernen.

1. ---	5. ---
2. ---	6. ---
3. ---	7. ---
4. ---	8. ---

10-10 Warum machen wir das? You and a friend are going on a trip. Renate has lots of questions about the trip. You will hear a series of questions followed by a cue. Using the cues provided, answer the questions in complete sentences using **um . . . zu**. You will then hear the correct answer. Repeat the correct answer after the speaker.

BEISPIEL: YOU HEAR: Warum kauft ihr Brot? (etwas essen)
YOU SAY: Wir kaufen Brot, um etwas zu essen.

1. ---	4. ---
2. ---	5. ---
3. ---	6. ---

10-11 Ich möchte lieber etwas Anderes tun. You will hear a series of questions, followed by a cue. Answer the questions affirmatively, and using **anstatt . . . zu** indicate that you are doing the first activity instead of the one in the cue. You will then hear the correct answer. Repeat the correct answer after the speaker.

BEISPIEL: YOU HEAR: Trägst du eine Jacke? (einen Pullover anziehen)
              YOU SAY: Ja, ich trage eine Jacke, anstatt einen Pullover anzuziehen.

1. ---
2. ---
3. ---

4. ---
5. ---
6. ---

10-12 Was macht Frank? You will hear a series of statements about Frank's activities, each followed by a cue. Indicate that Frank does the first activity but not the second one, using **ohne . . . zu.** You will then hear the correct answer. Repeat the correct answer after the speaker.

BEISPIEL: YOU HEAR: Er hat seine Tante besucht. (Blumen mitbringen)
              YOU SAY: Er hat seine Tante besucht, ohne Blumen mitzubringen.

1. ---
2. ---
3. ---

4. ---
5. ---
6. ---

The simple past tense

10-13 Wie war das früher? You will hear a series of sentences in the present tense. Change them to the simple past tense. You will then hear the correct answer. Repeat the correct answer after the speaker.

1. ---
2. ---
3. ---

4. ---
5. ---
6. ---

10-14 Berühmte Leute. You will hear a series of sentences in the present tense about the following famous people. Change them to the simple past tense. You will then hear the correct answer. Repeat the answer after the speaker.

1. Mozart
2. Columbus
3. Frank Sinatra
4. Mutter Teresa
5. Levi Strauss
6. Thomas Mann

7. Albert Einstein
8. Bertolt Brecht
9. Fritz Lang
10. Walter Gropius
11. Marlene Dietrich
12. Joe DiMaggio

10-15 Fragen und Antworten. Robert and Laura went to Germany on vacation last year. You will hear a series of questions. Answer each one affirmatively in the simple past tense. You will then hear the correct answer. Repeat the correct answer after the speaker.

BEISPIEL: YOU HEAR: Haben Laura und Robert Geschenke gekauft?
          YOU SAY: Ja, Laura und Robert kauften Geschenke.

1. ---
2. ---
3. ---
4. ---
5. ---

6. ---
7. ---
8. ---
9. ---
10. ---

da- and *wo*-compounds

10-16 Claudias Wohnzimmer. Claudia's friend is asking about the new arrangement of her living room. You will hear a series of questions. Answer each one using an appropriate **da**-compound. You will then hear the correct answer. Repeat the correct answer after the speaker.

BEISPIEL: YOU HEAR: Steht der Schreibtisch neben den Bücherregalen?
          YOU SAY: Nein, der Schreibtisch steht darunter.

1. ---
2. ---
3. ---
4. ---

5. ---
6. ---
7. ---
8. ---

10-17 Wie bitte? Emil went to a restaurant with a friend last week. You will hear a series of answers. Form the corresponding questions using **wo**-compounds or prepositions plus pronouns, as appropriate. You will then hear the correct answer. Repeat the correct answer after the speaker.

BEISPIEL: YOU HEAR: Emil erzählte von seinem Besuch im Restaurant.
                      YOU SAY: Wovon erzählte Emil?

1. ---   5. ---
2. ---   6. ---
3. ---   7. ---
4. ---   8. ---

Hörverständnis

10-18 Wissen Sie das? You will hear a series of questions. Listen carefully and respond aloud. You will then hear the correct answer.

1. ---   6. ---
2. ---   7. ---
3. ---   8. ---
4. ---   9. ---
5. ---   10. ---

10-19 Diktat: Die Schweiz. You will hear a short paragraph. It will be read once in its entirety, then again with pauses. Use the pauses to write what you have heard. You may listen to the passage as often as needed.

_____

_____

_____

_____

_____

_____

_____

_____

_____

10-20 Allein in einer großen Stadt. You will hear a brief passage about a student's travels. Listen carefully, then answer the following questions in complete sentences. You may listen to the passage as often as needed.

1. Wann ist Christa in Berlin angekommen?

_____

2. Warum konnte Christa Jens nicht finden?

_____

3. Welche Information hat sie von der Auskunft bekommen?

_____

4. Wie ist Christa zur Jugendherberge gekommen?

_____

5. Wie lange dauerte die Fahrt bis zur Jugendherberge?

_____

6. Wie war das Wetter?

_____

7. Wo hat Jens auf Christa gewartet?

_____

Kapitel 11

Studieren und arbeiten

Gespräche

11-1 Unsere Schulsysteme. Listen carefully to the first part of the conversation in **Schritt 2** from your textbook.

11-2 Der Studienplan. Listen carefully to the conversation in **Schritt 5** from your textbook.

11-3 Pläne für die Zukunft. Listen carefully to the first part of the conversation in **Schritt 7** from your textbook.

11-4 Wiederholen Sie! Now listen again to the first part of the conversation from **Schritt 7** and repeat each phrase during the pause provided.

Aussprache

11-5 Der *z*-Laut. Repeat each word after the speaker.

Zunge	Zahl	Zeit	Schweiz	Herz
Schmerzen	schmutzig	zehn	zwanzig	putzen

11-6 Der *s*- + Konsonant-Laut. Repeat each word after the speaker.

Stück	Spaß	spielen	Sparkasse	Spanien
Stadt	Stuhl	stellen	Straße	Sport
rasten	Komponist	Faust	Auster	gestern

11-7 Der *kn*-Laut. Repeat each word after the speaker.

knusprig	Knoblauch	Knoten	Knabe	knurren
Knebel	knicken	knacken	Knete	Knie

11-8 Der *pf*-Laut. Repeat each word after the speaker.

pfeifen	Pflanze	Pfeffer	Apfel	Topf
pfiffig	empfehlen	Pflaume	pflanzen	knüpfen

11-9 Zungenbrecher. You will hear a tongue twister. It will be read twice. The first time, just listen. The second time, repeat each phrase during the pause.

Im Zoo gibt es:
knurrende Katzen mit großen Pfoten,
gestreifte Zebras und pfeifende Spatzen,
kleine Knaben und Mädchen mit Zöpfen
und Spaß für die ganze Familie.

Strukturen

Verbs with prepositions

11-10 So viele Fragen. Astrid has joined your seminar very late in the semester and has lots of questions about the class. You will hear a series of questions. Answer them, using the cues provided. You will then hear the correct answer. Repeat the correct answer after the speaker.

BEISPIEL: YOU HEAR: Worauf freut ihr euch? (unser Urlaub)
               YOU SAY: Wir freuen uns auf unseren Urlaub.

1. ---		6. ---
2. ---		7. ---
3. ---		8. ---
4. ---		9. ---
5. ---		10. ---

The genitive case

11-11 Wem gehört was? You are at a Lost and Found identifying some items. You will hear a series of questions, each followed by a noun. Use the noun to reply to the question, using the genitive case. Repeat the correct answer after the speaker.

BEISPIEL: YOU HEAR: Wessen Buch ist das? (meine Schwester)
               YOU SAY: Das ist das Buch meiner Schwester.

1. ---		6. ---
2. ---		7. ---
3. ---		8. ---
4. ---		9. ---
5. ---		10. ---

Prepositions with the genitive

11-12 Wie bitte? You will hear a series of sentences, each read twice, then a cue. Insert the cue into the sentence, using the genitive preposition that is printed below. You will then hear the correct answer. Repeat the correct answer after the speaker.

BEISPIEL: YOU HEAR: Reinhard will die Zeitung lesen.
              Reinhard will die Zeitung lesen. (das Buch)
            YOU SEE: statt
            YOU SAY: Reinhard will statt des Buches die Zeitung lesen.

1. während
2. während
3. wegen
4. trotz

5. trotz
6. während
7. statt

Indefinite time / review of definite time

11-13 Sie haben Glück. You have the chance to do anything you like during the following time periods. Say what you would like to do using complete sentences. You may stop the recording while you respond aloud.

1. ---
2. ---
3. ---
4. ---

5. ---
6. ---
7. ---
8. ---

The future tense

11-14 Margaritas Leben ändert sich. Margarita is starting a new job. You will hear a series of sentences. Change them to the future tense. You will then hear the correct answer. Repeat the correct answer after the speaker.

BEISPIEL: YOU HEAR: Ich fahre mit dem Bus zur Arbeit.
            YOU SAY: Ich werde mit dem Bus zur Arbeit fahren.

1. ---
2. ---
3. ---

4. ---
5. ---
6. ---

11-15 Was ist denn mit Lothar los? Ursula is wondering about Lothar. You will hear a series of questions. Answer that the speaker is probably right. You will then hear the correct answer. Repeat the correct answer after the speaker.

BEISPIEL: YOU HEAR: Er ist krank, nicht wahr?
              YOU SAY: Ja, er wird wohl krank sein.

1. ---
2. ---
3. ---
4. ---

5. ---
6. ---
7. ---
8. ---

Nouns: Review and expansion

11-16 Wie sagt man das? You will hear a series of sentences, each followed by a noun. Substitute the direct object with the given noun. You will then hear the correct answer. Repeat the correct answer after the speaker.

BEISPIEL: YOU HEAR: Sehen Sie die Frau dort? (Herr)
              YOU SAY: Sehen Sie den Herrn dort?

1. ---
2. ---
3. ---

4. ---
5. ---

11-17 Was wollen Sie wissen? You will hear a series of sentences, each followed by a cue. Insert the cue into the sentence as an indirect object. You will then hear the correct answer. Repeat the correct answer after the speaker.

BEISPIEL: YOU HEAR: Was hat der Arzt gesagt? (der Kranke)
              YOU SAY: Was hat der Arzt dem Kranken gesagt?

1. ---
2. ---
3. ---

4. ---
5. ---
6. ---

11-18 Das Gute daran. You will hear a series of incomplete sentences. Give the correct form of the adjectival nouns **mein Verwandter** or **meine Verwandte** to complete the sentences. You will then hear the correct answer. Repeat the correct answer after the speaker.

1. ---
2. ---
3. ---

4. ---
5. ---
6. ---

Now use the correct form of the adjectival nouns **das Beste**, **die Beste**, or **der Beste**. You will then hear the correct answer. Repeat the correct answer after the speaker.

1. ---   3. ---
2. ---   4. ---

Hörverständnis

11-19 *Logisch* oder *unlogisch*? You will hear a series of statements. Circle **L** if they are logical, **U** if they are not.

1. L   U   5. L   U
2. L   U   6. L   U
3. L   U   7. L   U
4. L   U   8. L   U

11-20 Ein neues Semester beginnt. Two students, Felix and Brigitte, are discussing their new courses. Listen to their conversation then answer the questions. You may listen to the recording as often as needed.

1. Welche Kurse belegt Felix?

_____

2. Was muss Felix lesen?

_____

3. Was muss er in dem Kurs sonst noch machen?

_____

4. Welche Kurse macht Brigitte?

_____

5. Was muss sie schreiben?

_____

6. Worüber wird sie schreiben?

_____

7. Wohin geht Felix?

_____

8. Wohin geht Brigitte?

_____

Kapitel 12

Der Mensch und die Medien

Gespräche

12-1 An deiner Stelle würde ich einmal zu Hause bleiben. Listen carefully to the conversation in **Schritt 3** from your textbook.

12-2 Der Anrufbeantworter. Listen carefully to the conversation in **Schritt 6** from your textbook.

12-3 Ein neues Handy! Listen carefully to the conversation in **Schritt 8** from your textbook.

12-4 Wiederholen Sie! Now listen again to the first part of the conversation from **Schritt 8** and repeat each phrase during the pause provided.

Aussprache

Review of sounds

12-5 Der *r*-Laut. Repeat each word after the speaker.

richtig	traurig	Ferse	Irland
Frankreich	Reklame	perfekt	Arm
Russland	brauchen	Marmor	Wurst
Schrift	Reisebüro	Bürste	besser

12-6 Der *ä*-Laut. Repeat each word after the speaker.

hässlich	Wäsche	Dänemark	Getränk
Pässe	Fälle	Käse	Städte
Gäste	verständlich	hängen	Gespräch

12-7 Der *ö*-Laut. Repeat each word after the speaker.

möbliert	können	einlösen	fröhlich
Körper	Töchter	höher	möglich
löschen	öffnen	böse	gehören

12-8 Der *ü*-Laut. Repeat each word after the speaker.

wünschen	Gewürz	Gemüse	müde
hübsch	Sprüche	Hüte	Schüler
Mütze	glücklich	früh	süß

12-9 Zungenbrecher. You will hear a series of tongue twisters. They will be read twice. The first time, just listen. The second time, repeat each phrase during the pause.

Schwarze Bären hören leise Geräusche in den Büschen

Schönere, süßere Weintrauben wären im Supermarkt erhältlich.

Grässliche Frösche springen empört aus kühlen Sümpfen.

Strukturen

The present tense subjunctive and its uses

12-10 Ach, wenn er nur etwas anders wäre! Katharina wishes she could change a few things about her boyfriend. You will hear a series of sentences describing his behaviors. State how Katharina wishes he were different. You will then hear the correct answer. Repeat the correct answer after the speaker.

BEISPIEL: YOU HEAR: Er spielt jeden Tag Computerspiele.
YOU SAY: Wenn er nur nicht jeden Tag Computerspiele spielte!

1. ---	5. ---
2. ---	6. ---
3. ---	7. ---
4. ---	8. ---

12-11 Wenn mein Leben nur nicht so wäre! You will hear a series of sentences in which Xaver tells about all the problems in his life. Using **wenn nur** and the present subjunctive, state what Xaver says to indicate his wish that each circumstance were otherwise. You will then hear the correct answer. Repeat the correct answer after the speaker.

BEISPIEL: YOU HEAR: Meine Eltern geben mir kein Geld.
YOU SAY: Wenn meine Eltern mir nur Geld gäben!

1. ---	6. ---
2. ---	7. ---
3. ---	8. ---
4. ---	9. ---
5. ---	10. ---

12-12 Wenn . . . , dann . . . . You will hear pairs of sentences about Vera's life, each read twice. Use the subjunctive to state how the given consequence in the second sentence would be different if each condition expressed in the first sentence were untrue. You will then hear the correct answer. Repeat the correct answer after the speaker.

BEISPIEL: YOU HEAR: Vera hat keine Zeit. Sie sieht nicht fern.
　　　　　　　　YOU SAY: Wenn Vera Zeit hätte, sähe sie fern.

1. ---   4. ---
2. ---   5. ---
3. ---   6. ---

12-13 Ich wünschte, ... Your friend wishes certain things would happen, and you agree. You will hear a series of sentences. Restate them, using **wünschte** and the appropriate form of **würde**. You will then hear the correct answer. Repeat the correct answer after the speaker.

BEISPIEL: YOU HEAR: Wenn die Professorin nur anriefe!
　　　　　　　　YOU SAY: Ich wünschte, die Professorin würde anrufen.

1. ---   4. ---
2. ---   5. ---
3. ---   6. ---

12-14 Wäre das möglich? The students at your university are so impolite! You will hear some of their questions. Make them more polite by restating them using the subjunctive. You will then hear the correct answer. Repeat the correct answer after the speaker.

BEISPIEL: YOU HEAR: Kann ich hier parken?
　　　　　　　　YOU SAY: Könnte ich hier parken?

1. ---   5. ---
2. ---   6. ---
3. ---   7. ---
4. ---   8. ---

The past subjunctive

12-15 Rotkäppchen wäre am liebsten zu Hause geblieben. Little Red Riding Hood had a frightening day! If things had only gone differently, she might have avoided the traumatic experience with the wolf. You will hear a series of sentences. Use **wenn**-clauses and the past subjunctive to express how things might have been different. You will then hear the correct answer. Repeat the correct answer after the speaker.

BEISPIEL: YOU HEAR: Die Mutter hat sie zu ihrer Oma geschickt.
YOU SAY: Wenn die Mutter sie nur nicht zu ihrer Oma geschickt hätte!

1. ---   5. ---
2. ---   6. ---
3. ---   7. ---
4. ---   8. ---

12-16 Holger wünschte, ... Holger just returned from a miserable vacation in Mexico. You will hear a series of sentences describing his vacation. Use **wünschte** and the past subjunctive to state how he wishes things had been different. You will then hear the correct answer. Repeat the correct answer after the speaker.

BEISPIEL: YOU HEAR: Er hat die Pyramiden nicht gesehen.
YOU SAY: Er wünschte, er hätte die Pyramiden gesehen.

1. ---   5. ---
2. ---   6. ---
3. ---   7. ---
4. ---   8. ---

12-17 Wenn wir nicht zu Hause geblieben wären, ... You will hear pairs of sentences about Barbara and Karl's weekend, each read twice. Use the subjunctive to state how the given consequence in the second sentence would be different if each condition expressed in the first sentence were untrue. You will then hear the correct answer. Repeat the correct answer after the speaker.

BEISPIEL: YOU HEAR: Es hat geregnet. Wir sind nicht spazieren gegangen.
YOU SAY: Wenn es nicht geregnet hätte, wären wir spazieren gegangen.

1. ---   4. ---
2. ---   5. ---
3. ---   6. ---

12-18 Persönliche Fragen. You will hear eight questions. Answer them in complete sentences. You may stop the recording as you respond.

1. ---
2. ---
3. ---
4. ---

5. ---
6. ---
7. ---
8. ---

Relative clauses and pronouns

12-19 Wie bitte? You will hear a series of sentences, each followed by a cue. Use the cues to restate the sentences. You will then hear the correct answer. Repeat it after the speaker.

BEISPIEL: YOU HEAR: Das ist der Mann, der in Amerika wohnt. (Frau)
            YOU SAY: Das ist die Frau, die in Amerika wohnt.

1. ---
2. ---
3. ---
4. ---

5. ---
6. ---
7. ---
8. ---

12-20 Was meinst du? You will hear a series of sentences, each followed by a cue. Use the cues to restate the sentences. You will then hear the correct answer. Repeat it after the speaker.

BEISPIEL: YOU HEAR: Kennst du den Film? Sean Connery spielt in dem Film.
            YOU SAY: Kennst du den Film, in dem Sean Connery spielt?

1. ---
2. ---
3. ---
4. ---
5. ---

6. ---
7. ---
8. ---
9. ---
10. ---

12-21 Wessen? Several students are discussing their preferences. You will hear a series of sentences, each followed by a cue. Use the cues to restate the sentences with a relative clause in the genitive. You will then hear the correct answer. Repeat the correct answer after the speaker.

BEISPIEL: YOU HEAR: Hast du das Haus gefunden? Die Tür war rot.
            YOU SAY: Hast du das Haus gefunden, dessen Tür rot war?

1. ---
2. ---
3. ---

4. ---
5. ---

Review of verbs

12-22 Heute oder gestern? A friend is asking whether you are doing certain activities today. Answer that you did each thing yesterday, using the perfect tense. You will then hear the correct answer. Repeat the correct answer after the speaker.

BEISPIEL: YOU HEAR: Leihst du mir heute dein Auto?
YOU SAY: Ich habe dir mein Auto gestern geliehen.

1. ---
2. ---
3. ---
4. ---

5. ---
6. ---
7. ---
8. ---

Hörverständnis

12-23 *Richtig* oder *falsch*? You will hear a series of statements. Circle **R** if they are correct, **F** if they are not.

1. R   F
2. R   F
3. R   F
4. R   F

5. R   F
6. R   F
7. R   F
8. R   F

12-24 Petra und Hannes machen Pläne. You will hear a conversation between two students about their plans for the evening. Listen carefully to their conversation, then answer the questions below. You may listen to the recording as often as needed.

1. Wohin wollen Petra und Hannes heute Abend gehen?

_____

2. Was möchte Hannes lieber sehen?

_____

3. Für was für einen Film entscheiden sie sich endlich? Warum?

_____

4. Was wollen sie vor dem Film machen?

_____

5. Wo wollen sie sich treffen?

_____

6. Wann wollen sie sich treffen?

_____

Answer Key

Kapitel 1

1-11
1. ie
2. ei
3. ei
4. ie
5. ie
6. ei
7. ei
8. ei
9. ie
10. ie

1-18
1. S
2. P
3. S
4. either
5. P

1-20 Guten Tag! Hier ist Lisa. Ich bin in New York. Meine Telefonnummer ist acht – sechs drei – sieben vier – zwei neun. Es geht mir gut. Tschüs.

1-21 Alexandra: 18 29 37

Alex: 32 56 89

Michelle: 91 93 84

Oliver: 88 74 35

Karl ist krank.

Kapitel 2

2-5
1. front ch
2. back ch
3. back ch
4. front ch
5. back ch
6. front ch

2-10

1. S		6.	S
2. S		7.	P
3. S		8.	P
4. P		9.	P
5. P		10.	S

2-19 Mein Klassenzimmer

Mein Klassenzimmer ist schön. Da sind eine Tafel, zwanzig Stühle und drei Fenster. Wir haben eine Professorin und neunzehn Studenten und Studentinnen. Da lernen wir Deutsch.

2-20

	NAMEN	BERUFE
Rolfs Geschwister	1. Peter	Student
	2. Helga	Kellnerin
Brigittes Geschwister	1. Claudia	Lehrerin
	2. Doris	arbeitet nicht
	3. Herbert	Mechaniker

Wer ist oft verliebt?	Herbert
verlobt?	Claudia
verheiratet?	Doris

Kapitel 3

3-4
1. w
2. f
3. f
4. f
5. w
6. f
7. w
8. w
9. w
10. f

3-11
1. durch
2. gegen
3. ohne
4. für
5. um
6. ohne

3-15 Meine Familie und meine Wohnung

Meine Familie wohnt in Frankfurt. Wir haben eine Wohnung. Meine Eltern sind Lehrer. Ich heiße Heidi, bin Studentin und wohne in Heidelberg. Mein Studentenzimmer in Heidelberg ist klein. Mein Möbel sind schön. Die Couch ist braun und orange. Der Tisch ist schon alt und die Stühle sind auch alt.

3-16

KARIN HAT	KARIN MÖCHTE	ANDREAS MÖCHTE
ein Zimmer	eine Kaffeemaschine	ein Zimmer
eine Couch		einen Kühlschrank
einen Sessel		eine Kaffeemaschine
ein Radio		ein Stereo
einen Fernseher		zwei Sessel

Kapitel 4

4-8
1. 4.40
2. 11.10
3. 17.00
4. 10.25
5. 7.30
6. 12.45

4-10
1. ein Bücherregal
2. der Familie
3. den Kindern
4. dem Professor
5. eine Kamera
6. meiner Mutter
7. den Bleistift

4-19 Die Ferien

Erik möchte im Sommer nach Deutschland und Österreich fahren. Er ist fleißig und arbeitet im Juni und Juli. Seine Freundin Susie möchte auch mit ihm fahren, aber es ist teuer. Ihr Vater sagt ihr, sie muss zu Hause bleiben.

4-20
1. Klaus
2. am Donnerstag
3. Er läuft gern Schlittschuh und wandert gern.
4. Sie schenken ihm einen Rucksack.

Kapitel 5

5-9 1. weiß
2. kennen
3. kennst
4. weiß
5. weiß

5-15 1. S
2. S
3. I
4. S
5. I
6. I
7. S
8. I

5-17 Wo wohnt Frank?

Frank hat eine Wohnung in Graz. Er ist vor sechs Monaten eingezogen. Außer einem Bad und einer Küche hat die Wohnung vier Zimmer. Er teilt sie mit zwei Mitbewohnerinnen. Sie sehen oft zusammen fern und abends gehen sie aus. Franks Wohnung gefällt ihm sehr gut.

Kapitel 6

6-12 Die Gesundheit

Alle Menschen möchten gesund sein. Wir müssen gesund essen, sollen nicht rauchen, nur wenig Alkohol aber viel Wasser trinken. Wir möchten ohne Stress leben und keine Schmerzen haben. Die Gesundheit ist sehr wichtig. Ohne Gesundheit können die Menschen nicht lernen, nicht arbeiten und nicht spielen. Tun Sie mehr für Ihre Gesundheit!

6-13 1. U
2. U
3. L
4. U
5. U
6. L
7. U
8. U
9. L
10. U

6-14 1. falsch
2. richtig
3. richtig
4. falsch
5. richtig
6. falsch

Kapitel 7

7-13 Kennen Sie Heidelberg?

Heidelberg ist eine Universitätsstadt in Süddeutschland. Die Stadt ist nicht sehr groß. Sie hat 130.000 Einwohner. Heidelberg hat einen schönen Fluss. Er heißt der Neckar. Die Altstadt liegt am Fluss. Da findet man das Rathaus, interessante Museen und alte Kirchen. Die Universität existiert schon seit dem Jahr 1386. Die Stadt ist wunderschön. Besuchen Sie Heidelberg!

7-14 1. Die Fahrt dauert 45 Minuten.
2. Es gibt einen Dom und sechs Kirchen.
3. Heute ist das Holstentor ein Museum.
4. Das Rathaus ist am Marktplatz.
5. In der Breiten Straße sind viele Hotels, Restaurants und andere Geschäfte.

Kapitel 8

8-10
1. ü
2. ü
3. ä
4. ö
5. ö
6. ö
7. ö
8. ä
9. ü
10. ö
11. ü
12. ä
13. ü
14. ö
15. ä
16. ü
17. ä
18. ä

8-17
1. F
2. F
3. F
4. R
5. R
6. R
7. F

8-18
1. Sie möchte wissen, ob er ins Kino gehen möchte.
2. Er bekommt 30 Euro.
3. Er hat sein Handy bezahlt und hat Sportschuhe und eine CD gekauft.
4. Anke schlägt vor, er soll weniger telefonieren, weniger einkaufen oder sich einen Job suchen.
5. Ja, er kann mit, weil Anke bezahlt.

Kapitel 9

9-6
1. pf
2. ff
3. ff
4. ff
5. pf
6. ff
7. pf
8. ff
9. pf
10. pf

9-7
1. k
2. kn
3. k
4. kn
5. k
6. kn
7. k
8. k
9. kn
10. kn

9-18

	LISA	NATHAN
Salat	x	x
Kartoffeln	x	
Pommes		x
Nudeln		
Fisch		
Hähnchen		x
Schweinefleisch	x	
grüne Bohnen		x
Zwiebeln	x	
Mineralwasser	x	
Bier		x
Zitronensaft		

Kapitel 10

10-5
1. ei
2. ie
3. ie
4. ei
5. ei
6. ie
7. ei
8. ie
9. ei
10. ie

10-6
1. back **ch**
2. front **ch**
3. back **ch**
4. back **ch**
5. front **ch**
6. back **ch**
7. front **ch**
8. back **ch**
9. front **ch**
10. back **ch**

10-7
1. w
2. v
3. w
4. v
5. w
6. w
7. v
8. v
9. w
10. v

10-19 Kennen Sie die Schweiz?

Die Schweiz ist ein kleines Land südlich von Deutschland. Die Schweiz hat etwa sieben Millionen Einwohner. Touristen fahren dahin, um die hohen Berge und die schönen Seen zu sehen. Man kann dort schön wandern oder sich einfach entspannen. Da findet man auch elegante Uhren und leckere Schokolade. Reisen Sie in die Schweiz!

10-20
1. Sie ist spät abends in Berlin angekommen.
2. Es waren so viele Menschen auf dem Bahnhof.
3. Sie hat die Telefonnummer und Adresse von einer Jugendherberge bekommen.
4. Sie ist mit dem Bus dahin gefahren.
5. Die Fahrt dauerte 10 Minuten.
6. Es hat geregnet.
7. Er hat vor der Jugendherberge auf sie gewartet.

Kapitel 11

11-19
1. U
2. L
3. L
4. L
5. U
6. U
7. U
8. U

11-20
1. Er belegt Kunstgeschichte des 19. Jahrhunderts und deutsche Literatur.
2. Er muss das Werk "Faust" lesen.
3. Er muss zwei Referate halten und eine lange Semesterarbeit über "Faust" schreiben.
4. Brigitte macht Betriebswirtschaft und amerikanische Politik
5. Sie muss eine Semesterarbeit schreiben.
6. Sie weiß noch nicht, worüber sie schreibt.
7. Er geht nach Hause.
8. Sie geht zu einer Vorlesung.

Kapitel 12

12-23
1. R
2. F
3. R
4. R
5. F
6. R
7. F
8. F

12-24
1. Sie wollen ins Kino gehen.
2. Hannes möchte lieber einen Krimi sehen.
3. Sie entscheiden sich für eine Komödie, weil gerade keine Krimis laufen und weil ein Schauspieler, den Hannes mag, in der Komödie spielt.
4. Sie wollen noch etwas in einem japanischen Restaurant essen.
5. Sie wollen sich auf dem Marktplatz treffen.
6. Sie wollen sich um halb sechs treffen.